PRODUCING YOUR OWN

ORDERS *of* SERVICE

PRODUCING YOUR OWN

ORDERS *of* SERVICE

Mark Earey

Foreword by the Rt Revd David Stancliffe
Chairman of the Liturgical Commission

Church House Publishing,
Church House,
Great Smith Street,
London SW1P 3NZ

ISBN 0-7151-2001-8

Published 2000 for the Archbishops' Council and Praxis
by Church House Publishing

Second impression 2000

Typeset by Latimer Trend & Company Ltd, Plymouth

Printed by The Cromwell Press Ltd, Trowbridge, Wiltshire

Contents

Foreword

One of the key aspects of *Common Worship* is flexibility and choice within a common framework and structure. *Common Worship* has not introduced this pattern – many churches have been developing ways of using appropriate seasonal texts and other variety for many years, first with material from *The Alternative Service Book 1980,* and more recently with resources such as *Patterns for Worship*, *Lent, Holy Week, Easter* and *The Promise of His Glory*. However, *Common Worship* has integrated this resource material more closely with the authorized services of the Church, so that adaptability to the local context is not an afterthought but a key principle.

The availability of technology such as personal computers and photocopiers, and the advent of sophisticated software for word processing and desktop publishing has both fed and enabled this. It means that one of the ways of using this flexibility – the production of local editions of Church of England services – has become easier and more common than ever before. Many churches will be using some form of locally produced orders of service alongside the editions of *Common Worship* published by Church House Publishing.

However, to use this opportunity to its best advantage most of us could benefit from some help in terms of the practical skills, the technological knowledge and the liturgical instincts required. The Church has previously issued guidance about copyright and some of the basic principles. Here we have this and more, brought together with design tips, help with the decision-making process and practical hints.

All of this is entirely in keeping with the work of *Praxis*, which was set up by the Liturgical Commission in partnership with the Group for the Renewal of Worship (GROW) and the Alcuin Club to foster just this sort of practical approach. This book marks the beginning of a creative partnership between *Praxis* and Church House Publishing, helping to turn the best liturgical thinking into good liturgical practice.

I hope that this timely book will be well used as a practical help to the many people involved in the production of their own orders of service.

✠David Sarum

Chairman of the Liturgical Commission

What is *Praxis*?

Praxis was formed in 1990, sponsored by the Liturgical Commission of the Church of England, the Alcuin Club, and the Group for the Renewal of Worship (GROW). It exists to provide and support liturgical education in the Church of England.

Its aims are:

- To enrich the practice and understanding of worship in the Church of England;
- To serve congregations and clergy in their exploration of the call to worship;
- To provide a forum in which different worshipping traditions can meet and interact.

The name *Praxis* comes from the Greek word for action. It emphasizes our practical concerns and conveys our conviction that worship is a primary expression of the Christian faith.

Praxis runs an annual programme of day conferences and residential workshops around the country, organized either centrally or by *Praxis* regions (informal networks of diocesan liturgical committees).

You can find out more about *Praxis* from our web site: www.sarum.ac.uk/praxis/

For a copy of the *Praxis* programme and details of how to affiliate, contact the *Praxis* office:
Praxis,
St Matthew's House,
20 Great Peter Street,
London SW1P 2BU
Tel: 020 7222 3704
Fax: 020 7233 0255
Email:
praxis@stmw.globalnet.co.uk

Thanks to all the churches that sent in examples of their own orders of service:

- St John the Baptist, Stockton-on-Tees
- St Clement's, West Worcester
- St Luke's, Cranham Park, Essex
- Parishes of Bradford Peverell, Stratton, Frampton and Sydling St Nicholas, Dorset
- Parishes of Kinnerley, Melverley, Knockin and Maesbrook, Shropshire
- St Peter's Ipsley, Redditch
- Parish of Whitwell with Steetley, Worksop
- St Michael and All Angels, Hull
- St Andrew's, Countesthorpe, Leicestershire
- St George's, Altrincham, Cheshire
- The Oakdale Team, Dorset
- St Edmund's, South Chingford, Essex
- St Matthew's, Northampton
- St John the Baptist, Epping, Essex
- Parish of Monkwearmouth
- Egham Parish Church, Surrey
- St James, St Paul and Holy Trinity, Bushey
- St Andrew's, Earlsfield

Acknowledgements

Particular thanks for help with this book are due to Rachel Boulding and the staff at CHP and Church House, Westminster, and to Alison Earey, Tim Stratford, Jean Boulton-Reynolds, John Hadijoannou and Richard Curtis who read earlier drafts and made valuable comments.

Thanks are also due to those who sent in hints and tips and examples of their own local editions. They are listed on the left.

In addition, thanks are owed to the congregations of Christ the King, Chatham and St Mark's, Salisbury, who have been the guinea pigs for many of the ideas outlined here. The Durham Diocesan Liturgical Committee also provided valuable help through its *Common Worship* training materials.

A note about copyright

The Contracts and Copyright Administrator,
Church House Publishing,
Church House,
Great Smith Street,
London SW1P 3NZ
Tel: 020 7898 1557
Fax: 020 7898 1449
Email: copyright@c-of-e.org.uk

Preface – how to use this book

Pass it on

This book is designed so that key information can be passed on to those who will be able to make best use of it.

The best way to use it is for the person in the church who is responsible for producing orders of service to read through the whole book. Then certain sections can be copied and passed on to key members of the congregation who play different parts in the business of putting services together.

- Chapters 1 and 2 might form the basis of a PCC discussion;
- Chapters 3, 9 and 11 might be useful to the worship committee in putting together a proposal and overseeing production;
- Chapters 4, 6 and 8 might be helpful to the church secretary;
- Chapters 4, 5, 7, 8 and Appendix 1 might be given to all the worship leaders and those who produce orders of service;
- Chapter 10 could be passed to those who will proof-read the final text;
- Appendix 1 would be useful for those who operate the OHP during services.

Computer or not

Most of what is written here assumes that the reader has access to a fairly modern computer and printer, and is intending to use these for producing a local order of service.

However, not everyone has access to such technology and not everyone wants to use it. Much of the overall advice given here would also apply to producing a service sheet using a photocopier, scissors and glue (or indeed, a quill pen), but the detail will not always fit.

Where else to look

There is useful information in the following books:

Liturgical Commission, *Patterns for Worship*, Church House Publishing, 1995. Liturgical resource material, sample services and excellent advice on how to put a service together. Also includes the earlier version of A Service of the Word. A new edition of the book is expected within the next few years.

Trevor Lloyd, *A Service of the Word* (Grove Worship Series No. 151), Grove Books, 1999. Guidance on using A Service of the Word as the basis of your service (based on the newly authorized revised version).

Michael Perry, *Preparing for Worship*, Marshall Pickering, 1995. Useful tips about putting services together and writing your own texts, full indices of liturgical texts and guidance about printing orders of service.

Tim Stratford, *Worship and Technology* (Grove Worship Series No. 154), Grove Books, 1999. More thoughts on the impact of technology on the way we plan and lead worship. Raises both technological and theological issues and gives good advice.

General Synod, *A Brief Guide to Liturgical Copyright*, CHP. Detailed guidance about copyright and Church of England liturgy.

Robin Williams, *The PC Is Not a Typewriter*, Peachpit Press, 1992. Detailed advice on how to get the most out of word processing.

1 Introduction

A little history

As the twentieth century opened the Church of England's worship appeared on the surface to be exactly as it had been since 1662. However, though the printed words remained the same, at parish level there had always been variation from church to church and from decade to decade.

In the nineteenth century the Oxford Movement and the Anglo-Catholic revival highlighted some dissatisfaction with *The Book of Common Prayer*. Some churches began making alterations to the text of the service and adding a good deal of ceremonial and ritual which had previously been assumed to be illegal in the Church of England. The subsequent court cases and division within the Church led to the appointment of a Royal Commission, which reported in 1906 that, 'the law of public worship in the Church of England is too narrow for the religious life of the present generation'.

The first major attempt to change or supplement *The Book of Common Prayer* culminated in a new prayer book, which was rejected by Parliament in 1928 (and often referred to as the 1928 Prayer Book). However, it wasn't until the 1950s that the first Liturgical Commission was appointed.

The 1960s and 1970s saw a constant stream of revisions (Series 1, 2 and 3) which culminated in *The Alternative Service Book 1980*. The 1974 Worship and Doctrine Measure allowed the Church to make its own decisions about services which are alternatives to *The Book of Common Prayer*, without recourse to Parliament.

Why change again?

The natural way for worship to change is by a gradual evolution. The fixing by law of the liturgy (through the Act of Uniformity) meant that change and variety emerged in other ways. In some ways the recent and current revisions are the accumulated changes of four hundred years, happening in less than a century.

The only way to test liturgical material is to use it. The ASB was never intended to be permanent (as the 1980 in its title indicates). Many of the principles that lay behind the ASB have now been worked out more fully. Rather than simply extend its authorization for a further period, the opportunity has been taken to reflect on twenty years of use, to make some changes and to integrate it with the supplementary material that has emerged since 1980.

Different ways of thinking about worship

BCP – uniformity

National uniformity was the declared intention of liturgical policy in the sixteenth century. Seasonal variety was deliberately removed, in favour of simplicity.

The BCP was a 'local' form of worship in the sense that it was designed to be appropriate worship for England. The local flexibility built into our new *Common Worship* services is a developed form of the assumptions behind the Prayer Book.

ASB – flexibility

The ASB gave scope for some flexibility:

- It used phrases like 'using these or other suitable words';
- It included an element of choice (such as a selection of eucharistic prayers and forms of intercession);
- It included much more by way of 'propers' for different seasons and occasions – sentences, blessings, introductions to the peace, prefaces, etc.;
- It envisaged persons other than the minister taking part (reading scripture, leading intercessions, etc.).

Post-ASB – flexibility and variety

As well as continuing the provision for flexibility and local choice, the material published since the ASB has added a huge variety of seasonal material.

The 'right' way to worship is now seen as something determined more by context than by law. The most appropriate worship for a small congregation will not necessarily be the best for a large one; urban may not require the same as rural; an evening service may need different treatment from a morning one, and so on.

Common Worship

The new generation of liturgical material has the generic title *Common Worship: Services and Prayers for the Church of England*. The title itself tells us a lot:

- First, it is not a book. It is a collection of services and resources that will be published in books, as separate booklets, on simple cards, on computer disks and on the Internet.
- Secondly, it emphasizes the important part worship plays in expressing our unity.

The other key factor about the new services is that they have no 'sell-by' date. Unlike the ASB these services are authorized until it becomes obvious that it is time to think again – whether that is after ten years or one hundred. More significantly, this allows for each service to be considered separately so that, for instance, the baptism services could be revised without touching the communion services.

Common Worship will comprise a series of volumes which is expected to include the following:

- A main service book, called simply *Common Worship: Services and Prayers for the Church of England*, containing the major services and resources that might be needed on a Sunday or for other main acts of worship (including traditional language services);
- *Common Worship: Pastoral Services* – Marriage, Funerals, Wholeness and Healing, and Thanksgiving for the Gift of a Child;

- A volume of other resource material;
- *Common Worship: Daily Prayer* – liturgical material and a lectionary;
- An Ordinal – only preliminary work has been done on the revision of the Ordinal, so the ASB ordination services have had their authorization extended until 2005.

Separate service booklets will be produced for commonly used materials such as holy communion, funerals and marriage.

Principles behind *Common Worship* services

The *Common Worship* services by no means *require* locally produced orders of service on cards or in booklets, but they encourage the use of local editions by the way they are constructed. Some of the principles that are common to all the new services are:

- importance of structure and shape;
- flexibility, adaptability and local responsibility (essential for a church in mission mode);
- richness of language and seasonal variety;
- acceptance of the appropriateness of both modern and traditional forms;
- importance of making links between public worship, pastoral realities and private devotion;
- trying to preserve a 'family likeness' so that local services are connected both to the Church of England and to the wider church.

For more information about *Visual Liturgy* see Chapter 4.

The move towards localization of forms of service within a common framework and sharing some common texts has made it less and less feasible for a central publishing operation to provide all the permutations of services, seasonal variety and local flexibility that is necessary. In addition, both the possibilities and our expectations have increased greatly through the availability of new technology such as computers, copiers, the Internet, desktop publishing software and worship planning software such as *Visual Liturgy*.

However, great tools do not guarantee great quality work. The person who wasn't able to produce a decent looking order of service with a typewriter or with a photocopier, scissors and paste is not *necessarily* going to be helped by a laser printer and a copy of *Visual Liturgy*. Those producing local orders of service don't just need the technological tools; they need also to grasp some of the basic principles, to pick up some good advice, to learn some practical skills and to see what others have done. Then they need the discernment to apply all of that to the particular task in hand. This book is intended to help. Technology moves on and some of what appears here will soon be out of date, but the basic principles should be good for years to come.

Why bother?

The issue of why we might want to produce a local order of service at all is tackled in Chapter 2. However, it is wise to stop at this point and ask whether we really ought to be spending so much time and energy on producing better local orders of service. Many churches have been doing this for years – do we really need to wade through a whole book?

The vexed question of quality versus cost (in terms of money, time or energy) is one that the church grapples with all the time. For instance, do we really need church buildings, organs, banners, books or costly vestments? Many churches do without those things and the money could be spent in other ways. Yet there is another way of seeing things. A worship space is a statement of faith and an offering of creative gifts to God. Art, beauty, creativity are all things that have been valued in the Christian tradition as part of our worship.

For most of us the worship we offer to God in everything from music to vestments is a compromise between offering the very best (if we can agree on what that is) and offering what we can afford (which is often below the 'best' human standards). It is further complicated by the need to allow for worship to be offered by all Christians, young and old, rich and poor, talented and 'ordinary'. In the end we aim for 'good enough' in most of what we do. Not so shoddy that it dishonours God, but not so costly that it prevents or distracts us from offering the worship that truly pleases God – lives lived in love and service to him and to others. If this is true of other aspects of our worship, it is true also of the orders of service that we produce. A scruffy order of service may contribute to scruffy and unworthy worship.

Behind this book is a desire for locally produced orders of service that fulfil three criteria:

- They will do the job as well as possible, thus enabling people to worship God.
- They will do the job in an attractive and beautiful way, so that the order of service itself is an expression of love for God and others, and an offering of time and talents.
- They will do it without breaking the budget or the spirit, and without being so 'fancy' that they distract the worshippers.

2 Why print a local edition?

Official service books, properly printed and beautifully produced, have many advantages. They should last longer and, if the design is good, they should look pleasing to the eye and be easy to use. They normally contain all, or most of, the possibilities and therefore they allow for flexibility and a choice of texts within the service.

Service books also act as a symbol and reminder of the wider Church by including services that we may rarely use in our congregation, but which form the staple diet of other churches. Such service books can help us to feel that we belong to something beyond our local church and, if we encounter them when we visit another church, they can help us to feel at home. This symbolic role of service books in reminding us of the 'bigger picture' and the wider church is one reason why every Church of England church ought to have some copies of the official service books available, even if most services are led from local editions of some sort.

There are other reasons, too, why local editions won't meet every need. For instance, service books make a good resource for one-off (and possibly short-notice) occasions when there isn't time to produce something specially, and the locally produced service sheet isn't appropriate. If you decide one month to use Night Prayer at the end of the PCC meeting, your Parish Eucharist booklet won't be much use to you.

In addition there may be good reasons not to produce local orders of service:

- The published services may work perfectly well for the needs of the particular church.
- The regular and invariable use of a locally produced order of service may reduce the scope for flexibility and variety in worship.

- There may be issues about ecology and waste connected with producing 'throw-away' liturgy.
- There may be problems of cost, particularly if the church does not already have access to computer equipment and an economical means of bulk copying (see Chapter 9). A leaflet may be cheaper than a book, but a really nice leaflet will cost money, and if you are producing lots of different orders of service then the cost could mount.
- There may be the danger of work overload for those producing local orders of service.

But there are also disadvantages to relying solely on published service books:

- They can go out of date (as the ASB quickly did once inclusive language became an issue in the Church).
- They can seem complicated to use, especially to those who are not familiar with the service and (ironically) if the built-in flexibility involves skipping pages or using material in appendices.
- It can be necessary to give complicated instructions during the course of a service simply to make sure people know where you are in the book.
- Their sheer permanence can become a burden when a congregation wishes to make changes to its regular pattern of services.
- It can be very costly to buy enough for a whole congregation. This could turn out to be wasteful if in five years' time the congregation wishes to change its worship pattern and the books no longer serve that pattern well.

Technology has made it increasingly easy and economical for a church to produce its own order of service to suit its own patterns of worship. The fact that it is easy does not necessarily mean that it is right, but it does enable us to weigh up the pros and cons without being too constrained by cost or practicalities. For many churches the use of published service books (for instance, at an early morning Holy Communion service, or at Evensong), centrally produced booklets or cards (for a mid-week Eucharist, for instance) and the production of a local order of service (perhaps for an all-age service or parish Eucharist) will go hand in hand.

Advantages of a local order of service

Ease of use

Most churches have a 'regular' pattern for their services. They may make changes sometimes, or swap the order of some items, or cut out a hymn to allow for an extra item, but these are exceptions to a general rule. They will have a regular pattern for where the confession comes, what form it normally takes, when the hymns come and how many there are, and so on.

A local service booklet or card can give worshippers a clear path through the service. This saves the minister from having to call out page numbers and the congregation from getting lost as they jump from one section of the book to another, missing bits out one minute and using texts from an appendix the next. This straightforward path through the service can be particularly helpful for visitors and can help worshippers to concentrate on God rather than on which page to turn to next.

It can be particularly useful to print your own order of service if you happen to do things in a different order to the published service. For instance, in the *Common Worship* Holy Communion Service (Order 1), the penitential section is printed near the beginning. A note indicates that it may be placed later in the service (the note does not specify exactly where), but the officially produced books and booklets will not print it there. So, if your normal practice is always to have the Prayers of Penitence after the Intercessions and it is a practice you wish to continue, you are faced with a choice. You either have to skip the penitential material at the start of the service and then refer people back to it after the intercessions, or you can print your own order of service with penitence in the place where you use it.

Passing on practical information

Churches also have their own particular way of doing practical things, whether it is instructions about the way communion is distributed or directions to the toilets or information about the children's groups. All of this tends to be taken for granted by regulars but can be vital information for visitors. Printing it as part of your local service booklet can be a way of passing on the information to the visitors without boring the regulars.

Seasonal variety

There is much liturgical material available now that enables us to celebrate the seasons of the Christian Year more fully than was expected in *The Book of Common Prayer* or the ASB. Some (though not all) of that material is hard to use unless you can print it out for those in the congregation.

Mixing and matching

One of the key principles of the *Common Worship* services is that both traditional and modern liturgy have an appropriate place in the Church today. The main *Common Worship* volume includes both modern and traditional language services, and in some circumstances it will be appropriate to include both modern and traditional language texts within one order of service. For instance, a church using a modern language service of Holy Communion may choose to use the Prayer of Humble Access in traditional language. It is much easier to do this if you are using a locally produced order of service.

Appropriateness to the local context

Another key principle behind the flexibility built into *Common Worship* is the need for worship to be appropriate and relevant to local culture and needs.

It may be right for some parts of your Sunday service to be written by local people, or chosen by your church worship committee. A local edition enables these choices to be incorporated along with authorized material in one booklet, thus emphasizing that locally produced material is not second class. It also enables centrally produced material (over which much time and energy has been expended) to be used alongside more ephemeral, locally devised material. A local edition also allows for the inclusion of other local particularities: for instance, the normal use of a particular musical setting or of certain songs or hymns in the course of a service (though beware of the copyright implications – see Chapter 4).

Meeting particular needs

If someone finds it hard to read the print of a normal service, then the last thing they need is to have to find their way around a complicated book. A locally produced booklet can be easier to follow, and tends to weigh a lot less than large print books. It becomes easy and cheap to produce enough large print editions for all those who need them. (See Chapter 8 for more information on making print easy to read.)

At its most simple, an A5 size service booklet can be enlarged on a photocopier to A4 size. However, this may make the large print edition rather unwieldy and the user rather conspicuous. A more discreet and manageable solution is to produce the large print edition on the same size paper as the standard edition, but with more pages and the congregation's text in much larger print. Page numbers will be different, but the use of section numbers can reduce that problem.

For those with manual dexterity problems a small booklet or card is a lot easier to handle and use than a heavy book of several hundred pages.

Additionally, your church may want to have a special edition of your service for children to use, with larger print, fewer rubrics, some explanatory comments and some pictures – in fact, a lot of adults might appreciate those too!

Learning about worship

If you have produced your own order of service, it can be easy to add some comments and explanations so that people are helped to see the shape of the service and to understand what is happening and why. There is a danger of turning worship into RE, but the benefits can outweigh the dangers if care is taken.

See Appendix 2 Example 7 page 92 for an example of explanatory comments relating to the text.

Such comments could be incorporated into the margin of your order of service, or they could be included in a 'special edition' of the service which people can take home to read at their leisure. A children's edition might include large black and white line drawings and each child could colour in their own copy which they would keep at home.

Or your 'special edition' could be used for just part of the year – enough to get the benefit without the explanations dominating the worship.

Devotional connections

In the same way that local editions can incorporate teaching about worship, so they can also incorporate features that help make connections with the private devotions of the congregation, both at church and at home. A locally produced booklet could incorporate:

- prayers for use at home as part of preparation for Sunday worship;
- prayers to use while waiting for the service to start;
- devotional material for use during the service (for instance, during the administration of communion);
- resources for use at home after church (such as a grace for Sunday lunch).

For a season like Easter you might be able to print all the collects for the season on the inside cover of a service booklet. Or you might be following a six-week sermon series through the summer and produce a special order of service, with related prayers and readings for use at home. Again, all of this could be in the standard edition for use in church, or in a special edition that members of the congregation could purchase and keep at home.

Ownership and partnership

Though the official book may give a clearer sense of belonging to the wider Church, a locally produced service book can enable a sense that the worship belongs to the local church and is not simply 'imposed from above'. The use of standard headings, core Church of England texts and perhaps the Church of England logo can still help to give a sense of connectedness with the wider Church.

The production of a local booklet or card has the potential to involve lots of people:

- a worship committee, PCC or other decision-making body;
- someone to type in the texts, or to gather them from computer disk or Internet;
- someone with design skills to shape the way that it looks;
- those with artistic gifts to provide some illustrations (this could be a good way of involving the children of the church);
- the copier operator;
- those who do the collating, folding and stapling.

All of these people will have a sense that the service now 'belongs' to them.

However, it must be admitted that this collaborative way of working is not inherent to the production of a local order of service – it can just as easily become the job of the vicar alone, and a means of disempowering the laity. Making it a partnership requires real effort.

The back page could include some text such as:

> *St Gertrude's is the Church of England parish church of Bigtown and part of the diocese of Bigbury. This booklet has been produced by the people of St Gertrude's and falls within the permitted variations for a service of Holy Communion in the Church of England.*

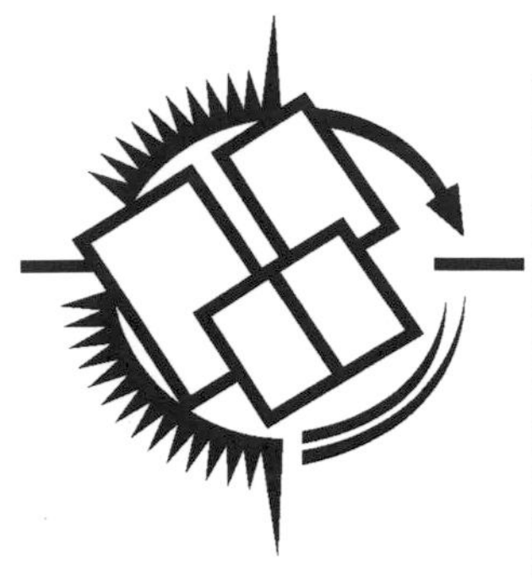

3 What sort of local edition?

It is one thing to decide to print your own order of service: it is quite another to find what will be the best sort of thing to produce.

Making a start – assess your needs

Go back to Chapter 2 and look at some of the reasons for producing a local edition. Which of them (if any) apply in your case? Are there any other factors or needs particular to your situation? If there are several reasons and needs, which is the key one? Will the others wait, or should you try to tackle all of them with this publication or series of publications?

Consider your options

There is a range of options for local editions. Here are just a few of the permutations.

A regular service booklet

This might contain the main service you use on a Sunday, or possibly a range of services including Holy Communion, all-age services and Baptism.

Is this to be an order of service, or would it work better as a booklet with a basic outline at the front and then a range of numbered resources at the back to which people turn when necessary? If the latter, will the resources include only spoken texts (such as prayers, confessions, creeds, a selection of psalms, etc.) or will you also include a selection of songs and hymns?

The length and regularity of use will affect practical matters such as type of paper and method of binding.

Seasonal booklets

As above, but with a shorter period of use and a clearer focus. A seasonal booklet could include some teaching material about the season and appropriate devotional material for use at the service or at home.

Service cards

These might be folded or A4 format and may also be part of a set covering the seasons of the Church Year. The space constraints will make the decisions about design, font size and options included crucial.

One-off services

Many churches produce personalized orders of service for a wedding or a funeral and sometimes for a baptism or Service of Thanksgiving for the Gift of a Child. Sometimes it is necessary to produce a one-off order of service for a civic service, a charity event, a confirmation or an ecumenical gathering. In each case, ease of use and accessibility is of the essence.

Weekly service sheets

Few churches would want to print out the whole service afresh each week, but many churches produce a weekly sheet that might include the hymns and songs, the collect, the readings and the words said by the congregation, including the parts that might vary from week to week (such as forms of confession or intercession and so on).

Supplementary cards

It may be that you are generally happy with the service books you are using, but you want to produce a simple supplementary card containing the words of the baptism service. This could also be achieved by printing the extra words on the notice sheet.

Overhead projector

It is possible that you could achieve some flexibility and variety by the sensitive use of an overhead projector or data projector, possibly supplemented by printed words on the notice sheet. See Appendix 1 page 75 for advice on using an overhead projector in worship.

4 Sources and copyright

Sources for liturgical material

Books

Books are the obvious place to start, and there are lots of them – not only 'official' liturgy books of the Church of England and other denominations but a whole range of other 'unofficial' material with only its quality to commend it.

Don't forget that even if you have permission to use copyright words, you may not have permission to photocopy them straight out of the book. Layout and typography, as well as words, are protected by copyright.

Electronic formats

Liturgy is increasingly available in electronic form. This is a great boon for the hard-pressed typist, but can lead to liturgical overkill – putting in all the options and making regular changes simply because it is so easy to do so.

At the time of writing the following plain text disks are available for Church of England liturgy:

- *Patterns for Worship*
- *Common Worship: Initiation Services*
- *Seasonal Disk* (containing much material from *The Promise of His Glory, Enriching the Christian Year* and *Lent, Holy Week, Easter*)

Further disks will be produced for the *Common Worship* services.

'Plain text' disks

Some Church of England liturgy is available on disk. The disks contain just the text in a popular word processing format and in rich text format (RTF), which is readable by a wide range of word processing software.

There are other providers of such material. For instance, you can find *The Book of Common Prayer* (on CD from Churchill Systems) and the *Common Worship* lectionary (on CD from Mowbray).

Beyond Anglican liturgy you can find a whole range of other services and resources (such as the 'Storecupboard' CDs and 'The Living Word' from Redemptorist Publications) and songs and hymns (such as the disk that comes with the latest edition of *Songs of Fellowship*). The list grows almost daily.

Liturgy software

Liturgy software is not just a source – it's also a tool. It helps with the work of choosing and arranging the elements of an act of worship. There are a number of programs that will help you to choose and display the words of songs and hymns, but for liturgy software the most well known and widely used is *Visual Liturgy: Service and Worship Planning Software*.

Visual Liturgy

Visit the *Visual Liturgy* web site at: www.vislit.com

You can also subscribe to the email discussion group via the web site.

Visual Liturgy is available from most Christian bookshops, or direct from Church House Bookshop, 31 Great Smith Street, London, SW1P 3BN
Tel: 020 7898 1301
Fax: 020 7898 1305,
or online from:
www.chbookshop.co.uk

Visual Liturgy has a number of 'templates' for regularly used services (for instance, *Common Worship*: Baptism of Infants). These give you the basic outline of the service, and if you tell the software the date of the service it can choose appropriate readings and collects from the lectionary. You then have the opportunity to customize – omitting some elements, selecting from optional material, adding extra prayers and songs, and so on. The service is displayed on screen in two columns: on the left the outline of the service in headings and on the right the full text of the service as you have planned it. You have a choice about what to output from this process. You could print a basic outline with hymn numbers for the choir, or you might want the readings and collect for the weekly sheet, or the full text to be turned into an order of service. It is possible to set up your own templates within *Visual Liturgy* which give only the elements of the service which you use in the order in which you normally use them.

For most purposes the easiest way to make use of the full order of service is to paste it into a word processor or desktop publishing program that will allow you to format it in your preferred styles, fonts and so on.

'Patch'

An improvement or repair to a program, often available for download from the Internet.

All of the *Common Worship* services will be produced in *Visual Liturgy* format as add-on modules and ultimately incorporated into the core of future versions of the program.

Visual Liturgy has a dedicated following, and a reputation for taking the views of users seriously, offering regular updates and 'patches' for the program posted on a special *Visual Liturgy* web site for free download. There is an email discussion group specifically for users of the program, and participants regularly swap hints, tips, questions and new templates.

Visual Liturgy was originally developed for the Church of England, but it is now also available for Methodists to use with material from their *Methodist Worship Book*.

For Roman Catholic material the *Liturgy Disk* developed by Churchill Systems and published by Geoffrey Chapman includes the major rites (with software to help you put them together) and the words of the hymns in the *Celebration Hymnal for Everyone*.

The Internet

There is a wealth of liturgical material available on the Internet, from official denominational sites to DIY liturgy sites run by individuals. Not all of it is good, of course, and some of it would not be authorized for use in Church of England services (for instance, eucharistic prayers from other sources), but it does open up another place to look for liturgical material.

All of the *Common Worship* liturgical material is put on the Church of England's web site as and when it is authorized and published.

For *Common Worship* liturgy visit the Church of England's web site:

www.cofe.anglican.org

Church of England material

Liturgical material in the Church of England generally falls into one of four categories.

The Book of Common Prayer

Prayer Book services are authorized permanently in the Church of England, and the copyright is vested in the Crown (see page 22).

Authorized services

This includes anything which is an alternative to something in *The Book of Common Prayer*. For instance, because there is an Order for Holy Communion in the Prayer Book, any other form of Holy Communion is alternative to it, and therefore must be authorized by General Synod. All of the services in the ASB fell into this category, which made the ASB not so much an alternative 'service book', as a book of alternative services.

Authorized material includes all of the following:

- All of the services in the ASB until 31 December 2000. Thereafter only the ordination services;
- Series 1 burial and marriage;
- *Common Worship: Calendar, Lectionary and Collects*;
- *Common Worship: Initiation Services*;
- *Common Worship: A Service of the Word*, including authorized affirmations of faith, confessions, absolutions and canticles. It will appear in the main *Common Worship* service book;
- All other *Common Worship* material requiring authorization, as and when it is authorized.

Canon B 5

'...the minister ... may on occasions for which no provision is made in *The Book of Common Prayer* or by the General Synod ... use forms of service considered suitable by him [sic] for those occasions...'

'All variations in forms of service and all forms of service used under this Canon shall be reverent and seemly and shall be neither contrary to, nor indicative of any departure from, the doctrine of the Church of England in any essential matter.'

Commended services

According to the canons of the Church of England, additional material (that is, material which does not have an equivalent in *The Book of Common Prayer*) may appropriately be chosen or composed by the minister if there are no other directions from the diocesan bishop.

Recently, a lot of 'additional' material has been provided by the Liturgical Commission. Such material does not need to be authorized, but instead has been 'commended' by the House of Bishops following a debate in General Synod.

Commended services include:

- *Lent, Holy Week, Easter*;
- *The Promise of His Glory*.

The new *Common Worship* liturgical material includes both authorized and commended material, sometimes within one package (such as *Common Worship: Funeral Services*). *Patterns for Worship* also includes authorized material (such as A Service of the Word, confessions and affirmations of faith) and commended material (such as the resource material for intercessions, thanksgivings, praise, etc.).

Unofficial material

Much commonly used material, such as *Celebrating Common Prayer* and *Enriching the Christian Year*, is neither authorized nor commended. Such material may, of course, be used as part of authorized or commended services at the discretion of the minister, but it has no more 'status' within the Church of England than any other collection of prayers, services and supplementary seasonal or thematic resource material produced by private enterprise.

Rubrics such as *'These or other suitable words'* allow the minister or other leader to exercise discretion in selecting or composing appropriate material.

Some material in Church of England services may be composed locally or chosen from any source, as long as the criteria in Canon B 5 are fulfilled.

Copyright issues

Copyright in the United Kingdom is covered by the *Copyright, Designs and Patents Act, 1988*. Any work is copyright if the author is living, or died less than 70 years ago (until 1995 it was 50 years ago). The typography and design of a book is copyright until 25 years after publication, which means that until that time you cannot photocopy the layout of the text from that book without permission.

Copyright in worship texts can seem complicated, and many well-intentioned church or worship leaders continue to break the law, week in, week out. Thankfully things have got much easier in recent years. Dealing with copyright relating to songs and hymns has been made much more straightforward (for some, but not all, songs and hymns) by the advent of Christian Copyright Licensing International (CCLI – see below). Similarly, for churches wishing to use Church of England liturgical texts the situation has been much clearer and easier to operate since 1988.

Useful resources for information about copyright law in the UK

Eric Thorn, *Understanding Copyright*, Jay Books, £6.50. Tel 01297 489826
A practical guide to the Copyright Act that covers all aspects of the legislation likely to affect the church, not just hymns and worship songs.

Copyright, Designs and Patents Act, 1988, HMSO £18.00
238 pages of legislation for the person who wants to know exactly what the Act states.

Church of England liturgical texts

A lot of people are still unaware that using copyright Church of England texts in local orders of service is very simple and straightforward. The rules changed in 1988 and made it much easier for local churches to reproduce Church of England texts in local orders of service, whether those services are for a single occasion or repeated use. Note that information about copyright and local reproduction found in ASBs and other books that were printed before 1988 will therefore be incorrect.

For permission to reproduce material from *The Book of Common Prayer* apply to: The Permissions Controller, Cambridge University Press, The Edinburgh Building, Shaftesbury Road, Cambridge CB2 2RU Tel: 01223 312393 Fax: 01223 315052.

Copyright in *The Book of Common Prayer* is vested in the Crown and administered by Cambridge University Press. However, they have agreed that Prayer Book texts included in other official service books may be reproduced in local editions that meet certain conditions that are outlined below.

Copyright in other Church of England services and texts is vested in the Archbishops' Council. This includes those services which have been authorized by the General Synod and those books of resources that have been 'commended' for use by the House of Bishops (see pp. 20–21 above).

Note that until 31 December 1998 copyright was vested in the Central Board of Finance so, again, be aware that copyright information found in Church of England books printed before then will be out of date.

The basic rule of thumb is that you can use any of these texts in your order of service as long as the following apply:

- It's for local use.
- You aren't going to sell it.
- You are not making more than 500 copies.
- The order of service (or equivalent) has the name of your church on it (and the date of the service, if it is a one-off).
- It carries this copyright acknowledgement: '[Name of book], material from which is included in this service, is copyright © The Archbishops' Council.' [NB This is the latest version – until 31 December 1998 the copyright was held by the Central Board of Finance]

Copyright acknowledgement for Church of England texts:

'[Name of book], material from which is included in this service, is copyright © The Archbishops' Council.'

Fuller details are found in the booklet *A Brief Guide to Liturgical Copyright* (which is an updated version of the earlier *Liturgical Texts for Local Use*). Any reproduction of

Church of England texts that meets the conditions stated in the *Brief Guide* may be made without an application for copyright permission and without payment of a fee.

Permission must be gained in advance for any reproduction that does not comply with these conditions. If you are in any doubt about whether your order of service falls within the guidelines, then get in touch with the Copyright and Contracts Administrator.

If you wish to give more detail about where the material has come from, remember that '*Common Worship*' is the generic title of the new material and not the title of a book. The main 'core' book containing material for Sunday worship (and major feast days) includes the eucharistic material and Sunday non-eucharistic material. Its title is *Common Worship: Services and Prayers for the Church of England* and **not** *The Common Worship Book*.

In addition, don't forget that if you are including other material whose copyright does not belong to the Archbishops' Council, you will need to gain permission from the copyright owner, or clarify that no permission or fee is needed for your use of that material.

A Brief Guide to Liturgical Copyright
Copies are available from Church House Bookshop, 31 Great Smith Street, London, SW1P 3BN
Tel: 020 7898 1301
Fax: 020 7898 1305,
or online from: www.chbookshop.co.uk
The text is also contained in the Help file of *Visual Liturgy 2.0*

Enquiries about copyright relating to Church of England texts and applications for permission should be addressed to:
The Copyright and Contracts Administrator, The Archbishops' Council, Church House, Great Smith Street, London SW1P 3NZ
Tel: 020 7898 1557
Fax: 020 7898 1449
Email: copyright@c-of-e.org.uk

Local musical settings

Authorized and commended material may be used in a music setting for a parish, team or group ministry, cathedral or institution without prior application for copyright permission to the Archbishops' Council and without payment of a fee. This is subject to certain conditions: the words must faithfully and accurately follow the official text; the copies must carry the name of the parish and must not be offered for sale or for use by others; the setting must include a copyright notice. Further details can be found in *A Brief Guide to Liturgical Copyright*.

Celebrating Common Prayer
The Society of St Francis is happy for churches to reproduce texts for local use, but they expect to be asked in writing for permission.

Other liturgical texts

The Church has got used to the idea that many songs and hymns are still copyright, and that musicians, writers and publishers should receive the appropriate payment for the use of their work, whether that payment is made on an individual basis or through some joint scheme. Such payment not only fulfils legal requirements, it is also a means of protecting the livelihoods of musicians and writers, and the investment of publishers in Christian music publishing.

Enriching the Christian Year Material may be reproduced for use on a single occasion or for an annual occasion (for instance, Mothering Sunday) without permission, but more frequent use does require written permission.

However, payment for the use of copyright liturgical texts is not so well established, nor is there (at present) any umbrella scheme covering several writers or publishers. The best advice is to read carefully the guidance about copyright printed in any book containing prayers or services that you intend to reproduce locally. Unless permission is clearly given for local reproduction for non-commercial use you will need to get permission in writing from the publisher or copyright holder.

For biblical texts the copyright is held by the publishers of each translation. Some copyright owners do not require application to be made in every case, but allow reproduction, subject to proper acknowledgement, for extracts below a specified word limit. Full details can be found in A *Brief Guide to Liturgical Copyright.*

Copyright in songs, hymns and music

For more information on CCLI visit their web site: www.ccli.co.uk

It also includes links to other sites relating to copyright and worship. Or you can contact them at:
PO Box 1339,
Eastbourne, East Sussex.
BN21 4YF
Tel: 01323 417711
Fax: 01323 417722.

Christian Copyright Licensing International

Christian Copyright Licensing International (CCLI) runs an umbrella scheme which now operates internationally and covers many (but not all) of the most popular modern songs and hymns that are still within copyright. Users pay a single annual fee based on the size of church (or equivalent) for the right to reproduce songs or hymns covered by the scheme. Each year they are required to complete a survey indicating which of the songs have been used. This information is used as the basis for the distribution of fee incomes to the respective copyright holders. Each church, individual or organization has a unique licence number, which must be included whenever songs covered by the scheme are reproduced.

There are now several licences:

The Church Copyright Licence

This enables you to make overhead transparencies, songsheets and songbooks, input lyrics on a computer, record worship services, and make arrangements of the music (where no published version exists). It does not give permission for the copying of music (see below).

The Ad Hoc Church Copyright Licence

This licence covers special events such as conferences, festivals, special meetings, weddings, funerals, and so on.

The Music Reproduction Licence

This *additional* licence allows you to photocopy the music of thousands of hymns and worship songs. However, it is worth noting that many major music publishers are not part of the CCLI scheme.

In addition there are equivalent licences to cover the reproduction of material for collective worship and religious services in schools.

The Calamus scheme

Like CCLI, the Calamus scheme enables a number of composers and music publishers to collect royalties for the copying of their material in a centralized and simplified way by means of a single annual payment. Licences are available for churches and for schools. They are also able to deal with requests for permission for individual songs to be included in local songbooks and for reproduction for a single occasion.

Calamus covers Decani Music, Christopher Walker, The St Thomas More Group, Oregon Catholic Press, Clifton Music, GIA Publications Inc, North American Liturgy Resources and McCrimmons, among others.

Every item reproduced under the conditions of the CCLI scheme must include an acknowledgement.

For an individual song on paper or OHP:

'Reproduced under CCLI Licence No. 12345'

For an order of service or song book including several songs:

'Songs covered by the CCLI are reproduced here under Licence No. 12345'

Calamus

30 North Terrace,
Mildenhall, Suffolk,
IP28 7AB.
Tel/Fax: 01638 716 579.

Acknowledgements should normally come at the end of an order of service and would normally be much smaller than the rest of the text – perhaps in 8 point.

Looking for the '©' symbol?

It is there on your computer somewhere, but you won't find it on the keyboard.
Each word processing software program is different, but try looking under a menu such as 'Insert' and then select 'Symbol'. From the selection choose the ©.
If you can't see anything like this, see what the manual or onscreen Help can suggest if you look up 'symbols'.
You could also try typing '(c)'. Some word processors are clever enough to correct this to © automatically.

Acknowledging sources

Getting copyright permission (or establishing that you already have such permission by default) is only half the problem. Most copyright schemes require you to acknowledge your sources and the copyright holder, even if you don't have to get special permission to reproduce the item. More to the point, it is disrespectful not to do so.

Make sure you leave space on your order of service for acknowledgements. They normally come at the end of the service, as this prevents the 'look' of the service being disrupted and cluttered by copyright information. Try to ensure that the copyright and other acknowledgements do not look like the most important part of the service.

5 Some liturgical principles

The Golden Rule

The most important principle to have in mind when designing a local order of service is that what is produced should enable and free the people to take part in the event of worship: it should not turn them into spectators.

An order of service is not like a programme for a show: it is like an outline script for the actors. But even as a script it is a means and not an end and should not result in an obsession with the text, but in participation in the action.

Balancing the local and the universal

The Church of England works with a balance in its worship between local flexibility and national coherence. In this way the local congregation is enabled to take responsibility for itself without ever forgetting that worship is something bigger than 'the way we happen to do things here'. Though individuals will always find things in the authorized services with which they disagree, all of those services have been through a lengthy process of drafting and revision in order to take into account the needs of, and feedback from, a wide range of people. The result may not be perfect but it ought not to be disregarded lightly. A local edition should be recognizable as a version of the Church of England's agreed services, structures and texts. Local printing offers the chance to use those structures and texts creatively and in appropriate ways, but not to 'go it alone' as if the rest of the Church doesn't matter.

It can be helpful to ask yourself the question: 'Would a visiting Christian recognize from our order of service that we consider ourselves part of the Christian church around the world and down the centuries?'

Making the decisions

It follows from the above that one of the key principles from a liturgical point of view is, 'Who will make the decisions?' The Church of England's worship is intended to belong to the whole church rather than to the local vicar or congregation. However, this is not the same as saying it belongs to the General Synod or the Liturgical Commission.

Any Church of England service should have a sense of being owned by people other than the minister. Those 'other people' could include Christians from other denominations, Anglican Christians from other congregations, and the rest of the congregation.

Decisions about which forms of service are to be used generally in a parish should be taken 'jointly by the minister and the parochial church council' (Canon B 3.1). This lays down a collaborative principle and a shared responsibility that forms a good model for all decision-making in the church. Some churches will have a worship committee (which may or may not be a sub-committee of the PCC) and/or a ministry or worship leaders' team which might include all those who play a part in the leadership of worship in that church. These bodies will all have relevant input to decisions about locally produced orders of service, from questions of principle down to the detail of how they will be laid out and used.

'First, a clear structure is essential. Its main components should stand out so that worshippers can see the shape, development and climax of the service – so that they 'know where they are going'. It is helpful if this is reflected in the way the service is laid out for printing.'

Patterns for Worship, p.11

Getting the structure right

The importance of a clear sense of structure is one of the key liturgical principles underlying recent liturgical thinking and reform. All of the *Common Worship* services begin with a page or two on which the outline structure of the service is printed. This can be a great help in seeing the overall shape and the section headings and titles of the different elements. Structure is also seen as a major factor in preserving a sense of 'family likeness' for Church of England worship.

Only once you are clear about the structure should you begin to make choices about the texts. The starting point for both structure and text will be the published editions.

Using headings

The use of headings can be a major help in making clear the structure of the service. In all officially published services the hierarchies of headings, prominence of typeface and terminology used have been carefully considered. Local editions ought to reflect this and only deviate from them for good reason.

See Appendix 2, especially Examples 2 and 3, pages 82–5.

Think carefully before choosing headings – they give subtle (and not-so-subtle) clues about your congregation and how you perceive yourselves. Headings such as 'We gather', 'We listen', 'We break bread' and 'We share' would give a very different impression from 'The Gathering Rite', 'The Synaxis', 'The Penitential Rite' and 'The Anaphora'.
Each could be appropriate in the right circumstances. What you use will say something about your church and what you think you are doing in your worship.

What to include

Full text or congregational part only?

Sometimes it is appropriate to include the full text of a service for everyone to follow. On other occasions it may be more appropriate to include only the words said by the congregation.

Some of this material is based on advice found in the booklet *A Brief Guide to Liturgical Copyright.*

Full text

The advantage of a full text is that it is easier for the congregation to follow the service and find their place. Many people like to be able to follow for themselves what the minister is saying.

Congregational text only

For example, here's part of the eucharistic prayer:

Let us give thanks to the Lord our God.
It is right to give thanks and praise.

The president leads the Thanksgiving for the work of Christ, ending
... for ever praising you and saying:

Holy, holy, holy Lord,
God of power and might,
heaven and earth are full of your glory.
Hosanna in the highest.

The words of Christ at the supper end
... in remembrance of me.

Christ has died:
Christ is risen:
Christ will come again.

Congregational text only

The advantage of printing only the congregational text is that it allows for greater flexibility in the leader's words. For instance, printing only the congregational responses in the eucharistic prayer enables a variety of eucharistic prayers to be used with the same printed order.

It also takes up less space, making it possible to think in terms of a service card, perhaps, rather than a multi-page booklet. In addition, it encourages people to look up and to participate visually in the action rather than to bury their heads in the text.

However, for Anglicans there is a deeply ingrained expectation that the congregation should have access to the same text as the minister. Printing only part of the text may irritate some of the congregation, or even arouse suspicions of a hidden agenda. It may simply need careful explanation when the orders of service are introduced. It is also true that some people find it confusing to have some of the words printed on the card, but not all of them.

If a text is regularly varied it is best not to print it in the order of service unless it is accompanied by a clear note to that effect. For instance, if the pattern of words used at the intercessions varies completely depending on who is leading them, it is best to print only the regular response,

Lord, in your mercy,
hear our prayer.

and perhaps the final response and not to print any 'standard' form of text that may come in between.

Whichever you choose, this decision will affect the page layout and number of pages of your order of service. Conversely, if these are predetermined, this fact will affect decisions about how much of the minister's text is printed.

If you decide to print only the congregation's words, ensure that you include 'rubric text' which makes it clear what will happen in between. This will help the congregation to be ready to come in with their part.

Omissions from published texts

Authorized Church of England services make clear which sections are mandatory and which are optional. Mandatory sections may still have alternatives attached. In commended services the relative importance of the sections is indicated in the notes and rubrics.

The following may be omitted in locally produced orders:

- The notes relating to the service;
- Alternatives not required by the parish.

In addition, rubrics may be radically simplified, so long as they continue to reflect the intentions of the published text with regard to mandatory sections.

Making choices

Since *The Alternative Service Book 1980* we have got used to the idea of having choices about what we include in services and which form of words we use at various points. A good rule of thumb is that *having* a variety of options doesn't mean you have to give yourself all those options *every* time.

When we commit ourselves to print we inherently cut off some of those options, or at least, make it harder to use them. Sometimes we decide to print a local edition in order to give ourselves more choices (perhaps we want to print more than one creed or affirmation of faith in our order of service at the point at which it is used). Sometimes we want to make things simpler, perhaps only printing one eucharistic prayer because it's the one we use most often.

When making choices about what to include in our order of service we need to bear in mind that every choice we make will have an impact on how easy the service is to follow and on how much flexibility we will have in leading it. As a general rule, it is easier from the congregation's point of view, and from the point of view of producing orders of service, if the variety is built in across the *year* in a series of seasonal orders (rather than as an option every week) and the service order is kept fairly straightforward. You will want to avoid having to make announcements like, 'We will now use the second of the five confessions ...'! You might be able to use the notice sheet or an overhead projector to make odd one-off changes.

You might, however, want to build in *some* choices, especially for an order of service that you are going to be using very regularly, such as an order for Holy Communion for Ordinary Time. In that case it might be worth putting in an alternative confession, and perhaps a choice of creed or short affirmation of faith.

These are some of the things to bear in mind as you make choices:

- The opportunity for freshness and variety;
- The need for some familiarity (making 'internal' connections for the congregation);
- The expression of wider unity (making 'external' connections with the wider Church);
- Simplicity of use.

One way of combining simplicity with flexibility is to divide the service in two with each piece on a separate card. The obvious example is a service of Holy Communion. The split could come after the Peace, with a range of cards for both Part 1 and Part 2. All the Part 2 cards would be the same colour.

Only two cards are given out at the service, combining a Part 1 and a Part 2. The Part 1 card could finish with the instruction: *Please turn now to the [yellow] card.*

In this way you could provide a range of Part 1s with different emphases (e.g. penitence in different positions) and a range of Part 2s with different eucharistic prayers, alternative post-communion prayers, some including the Prayer of Humble Access, etc. A variation on the theme might be to print the main service on one card and a range of eucharistic prayers on other cards.

Rubrics and instructions

A lot of care has been taken over the wording of rubrics and other instructions in *Common Worship* – on the whole it is probably wisest to stick with these unless there is good reason to change them for your situation.

Many of the principles that apply to the choices made about the spoken text apply also to the rubrics and instructions.

See Appendix 2, Examples 1 and 8, pages 80–81 and 94–5.

In general, the more you print, the easier it will be for the visitor because fewer announcements have to be made. On the other hand, the page will begin to look cluttered and the rubrics will take up valuable space.

In a part of the service where you would prefer not to make a verbal announcement, a printed rubric is ideal. For instance, if you stand for the eucharistic prayer and then sit for the Lord's Prayer, a printed instruction saves an announcement at a particularly sensitive moment, but at points where you need to make an announcement anyway, it leaves your options open if you don't print anything. For example, if you are going to announce a hymn number you could also invite the congregation to stand. You don't necessarily need to print that instruction in the order of service as well – and you may be glad you didn't on the occasion when you decide it's more appropriate to remain seated to sing.

Always check that the rubrics are unambiguous and that they will make sense to someone who doesn't *already* know what you mean. Try them out on a range of people before going into print.

A convention that the congregation's words are always in bold can save a lot of rubrics, but sometimes we need to give more information. For instance, in a baptism service some of the text will be spoken by the minister, some by the parents and godparents or the candidate, and some by the whole congregation. In a situation where most of the congregation are unfamiliar with church (such as at a wedding or an afternoon service of baptism) it may be necessary to be even more specific.

It is worth giving some thought to how concise (or not) to make your rubrics. For example:

We stand for the gospel – long, but friendly in tone
We stand – concise, but still sounds like gentle guidance
All stand – clear, but reminiscent of a courtroom
Stand – concise and uncluttered, but looks more like an order

Do the rubrics make sense?

This rubric is slightly misleading:

The reader ends by saying:
This is the word of the Lord
Thanks be to God.

This version makes it slightly clearer that we all say some of the words:

After the reading this response is used:
This is the word of the Lord
Thanks be to God.

Being crystal clear:

The minister says
Praise God, who made heaven and earth.
We all say
Who keeps his promise forever.

Being clear about roles

In published services great care is taken about the way the rubrics allocate parts of the service to particular leaders. In local editions the rubrics should follow the published text unless there is good reason not to.

President

This means the overall leader of the service. Any service (eucharistic or not) may have a 'presiding minister' when the leadership is shared. However, in the Holy Communion the term always refers to the presiding priest. Some parts allocated to the president may be delegated to another minister (such as the collect) and others may not (such as the eucharistic prayer). See the notes attached to *Common Worship: Holy Communion* for more detail.

Priest

This may or may not be the president, but must be an ordained priest.

Deacon

There are no parts of the service that must be said by a deacon, but rubrics and notes may suggest certain parts of a service as appropriate for a deacon to lead.

Minister

This refers to any person leading that part of the service, lay or ordained.

For more on the principles of inclusive language as it relates to language about men and women, see the Liturgical Commission's report, *Making Women Visible*, Church House Publishing 1988.

Language issues

Inclusive

'Inclusive' language (meaning, in this case, trying to use language that does not make any group of people feel excluded) is a subject that is a burning issue for some people and leaves others cold. It most obviously relates to phrases that can be heard to exclude women, but that is not the only application of the principle.

The ASB was produced just before these issues came to the fore, and therefore contained lines about, 'fellow men', and so on, that would not be written today.

We all know that phrases like that are meant to cover both men and women, using language in a way that has been common for many generations. However, language is not always heard in the way it is intended, and even if we know what we mean, visitors may not. Hence all new Church of England liturgical texts are written to be as inclusive as possible. It is wise to follow the same principle with texts that are composed or chosen by the local church.

The issue of language about God is separate but related. The Church of England's position at the moment is to seek to use a wide range of modes of address to God (not just 'almighty') and to use the full range of biblical imagery for God, including the more feminine, such as God compared with a mother (Isaiah 66.13). However, there is no attempt deliberately to exclude traditional forms, such as God our Father. In some of these matters the conversation includes our ecumenical partners who are struggling with the same issues and sometimes come to different decisions.

Modern and traditional

When the ASB was published it was generally accepted that modern and traditional language was best kept separate: ASB for modern language services and BCP (and ASB Rite B, which slipped into the ASB at the last minute) for traditional language. The result has been an unnecessary division in the Church and a nervousness about hidden agendas behind liturgical reform. It was not many years after the ASB that the General Synod agreed that all new printings of the ASB should include the modern and modified traditional versions of the Lord's Prayer in parallel columns wherever it occurred.

The *Common Worship* services include as a matter of principle the idea that traditional and modern texts can be mixed within an order of service where it is appropriate and care is taken. Decisions about traditional texts (and especially matters such as the Lord's Prayer) tend to arouse a good deal of strong feeling. It is particularly important to take great care over how decisions are taken about versions of such well-known texts. A locally produced edition can be the opportunity to try out new versions in a short-term, experimental way. It can equally provide the opportunity to give choices and therefore variety, or to reinforce an existing pattern. Handle with care!

6 Basic word processor technique

Some of what follows is really basic. Some of it is a bit more sophisticated. Some of us are still being weaned off typewriters and find word processing software a new experience needing some new skills. But even if you have been using word processors for years, there just might be a nugget of new information hidden in here, so don't skip ahead too soon ...

One space between sentences

Typewriters needed two spaces between sentences. On a computer the letters are proportionally spaced, so that an 'i' takes up much less space than a 'w'. Hence, the letters sit closer together and each word is more distinct. This makes it easy to tell where the gaps are between sentences and so we don't *need* two spaces any more. In fact two spaces make it look as if the sentences are not on speaking terms and leaves big white gaps in blocks of text.

Tab or indent when aligning text

When you are just putting the finishing touches to the text and some lines don't seem to align properly, always seek the reason for the problem and stick rigidly to aligning using the tab key or indents. The space bar is an unreliable tool for aligning lines of text: it may look perfect on the screen, but the printer will reveal a different story.

Use 'style' definitions

Most modern word processing software allows you to assign a 'style' to any block of text. So you might have a style which you call 'Block Text' and another which you call 'Headings'. You can then define the style so that whenever you apply the 'Headings' style to some text it makes it larger and bold.

Within an order of service you might want to define several styles:

- minister's text
- congregation's text
- rubrics and notes
- section headings (such as 'Liturgy of the Word')
- titles (such as 'The Peace').

Defining and using these styles makes it much easier to make changes and to try things out. Imagine you want to change the font for headings. Without setting a style for headings you would have to go through and make the changes to each heading individually. Imagine you then changed your mind! If you set a style instead, you simply make a change to the definition of that style (perhaps size or font) and it is applied to every bit of text defined as 'Heading'. Or perhaps your order of service has lots of lines that are just too long for the column width and you want to see the effect of reducing the font size by one point on just the minister's text. By changing the 'Minister's text' style definition you can see instantly the effect of reducing the font size not only on one particular prayer but on the whole service, including where the page breaks come and how many pages the service would now take up.

It is worth taking the time to explore your software manual or the onscreen Help to find out how to do this in your program.

Appropriate paragraph settings

Word processors allow you to specify the characteristics of each paragraph (or of a paragraph 'style' – see above). This might include specifying how much space to leave before the start of the paragraph and how much to leave at the end.

For blocks of text it is often appropriate to set the paragraph to leave 6 points of space between each paragraph. This would work well for rubric text, but is a problem for spoken text, which is going to be split into short lines. The software will treat each of those lines as a separate paragraph (because each has a 'hard return' at the end). The result is very spaced out liturgy (as it were!). Make sure that the paragraph style for congregational text is set to leave no space after or before paragraphs. Alternatively, some word processors allow you to insert a 'soft return' or line break rather than a full paragraph break. This means that a new line will not be treated as a new paragraph, and is useful for setting liturgy, verse and addresses. Consult your software documentation.

Sensible hyphenation

Most word processors will put hyphens into your text automatically when a long word straddles the right margin. Hyphens should be avoided in liturgical text – instead, introduce a turn-over, where the sentence continues on the line below with an extra indent from the left margin. (See also Chapter 8.) You can either turn off the auto-hyphenation feature, or make the 'hyphenation zone' much larger.

Because turn-overs have to be introduced manually, they don't change when you make other changes to the text (changing font size, for instance) and so special care is needed at the proof-reading stage to make sure they are still appropriate.

Avoiding hyphens

Don't hyphenate, like this:

as we forgive those who trespass against us.

Use a turn-over like this:

as we forgive those
who trespass against us.

Avoid underlined text

Underlining was a great way of adding emphasis to handwritten or typewritten text, but it looks very messy and, nowadays, tends to look rather old-fashioned.

When you use the underline feature on a typewriter or word processor, the line that is drawn cuts through the 'descenders' of letters (the parts that go beneath the line, like the tail on a 'g'). If you want to add emphasis (to make a heading stand out, for instance), use bold or italic or a larger size. If you really want a line, don't use the underline function, but draw a line instead (if your word processor includes some drawing

Avoid using underlining

Underlining like this looks messy

Instead, use a drawn line:

This gives more scope

See Appendix 2, Example 4, page 86.

tools). Then you can put the line further below the text, preserving the descenders. You also have more control over the line thickness and style.

Some word processors also allow you to specify a line above or below the text (or, indeed, as a box all round the text) as part of the text's style definition.

Watch out for auto-correct

With a typewriter you had to press return at the end of every line. With a word processor the computer knows when you get near the right hand side of the page or column and moves to a new line on its own – you don't need to press return except at the end of a paragraph.

However, in liturgical text the lines are short, and so we do need to press return (or insert a manual line break) at the end of each line, even if the sense carries over onto the next line. Some software is so clever that it can automatically change the first letter of a new line to a capital. This is very helpful when you are writing a parish magazine article, but not when you are typing a service. Remember to turn this clever 'auto-correct' feature off before you start (consult your software manual or onscreen Help to find out how to do this). Otherwise you will end up with liturgy that looks like junior school poetry, with a capital letter at the start of every line.

7 Page layout options

For economy and ease most of us will be using A4 size paper. But how to use A4? There are several possibilities and before beginning to put a service together it can help to have them in mind.

A5, single column

A4 folded into A5 is probably the most obvious way of using an A4 sheet of paper for an order of service.

This is the orientation that works best for orders of service that use more than one sheet of paper (i.e. booklets rather than single sheets).

A5, two columns

Keeping the orientation the same but putting the text into two columns can dramatically increase the capacity of a single sheet of A4 paper. However, it is a bit limiting and looks fairly cramped for an order of service you are intending to use regularly.

The tables on the following pages outline the pros and cons of each format.

A5, single column

For	• Lots of white space gives a 'spacious' look which is easy on the eye and makes the service easy to follow. • Works well for 'booklets' as well as leaflets. • Space for margins, if you need them for instructions like, 'Candidate', 'Minister' and so on. • More room for pictures, symbols, clip art, etc. • Long lines can remain unbroken even with a larger font.
Against	• Takes up more paper – more likely to become a booklet rather than a single sheet. • A5 size is too large to sit easily on some pew ledges.
Good for ...	• Frequently used services, such as Parish Communion or Family Service. • Short services, such as Thanksgiving for the Gift of a Child.

St Gertrude's Church
PARISH COMMUNION

THE GATHERING

At the entry of the ministers a hymn may be sung.

Grace, mercy and peace
from God our Father
and the Lord Jesus Christ
be with you
and also with you.

PRAYER OF PREPARATION

This prayer may be said

Almighty God,
to whom all hearts are open,
all desires known,
and from whom no secrets are hidden:
cleanse the thoughts of our hearts
by the inspiration of your Holy Spirit,
that we may perfectly love you,
and worthily magnify your holy name;
through Christ our Lord. Amen.

PRAYERS OF PENITENCE

Our Lord Jesus Christ said: The first commandment is this: "Hear, O Israel, the Lord our God is the only Lord. You shall love the Lord your God with all your heart, with all your soul, with all your mind, and with all your strength."
The second is this: "Love your neighbour as yourself." There is no other commandment greater than these.
Amen. Lord, have mercy.

A5, two columns

For	• Very efficient use of space – you may be able to get the whole service on one sheet of paper.
Against	• Need to use a small font to avoid lots of line breaks. • Not much scope for 'white space' on the page, and therefore can look cramped. • No space for margins, if you need them for instructions like, 'Candidate', 'Minister' and so on. • A5 size is too large to sit easily on some pew ledges
Good for …	• One-off services, or those that are used infrequently or annually. • Paper shortages!

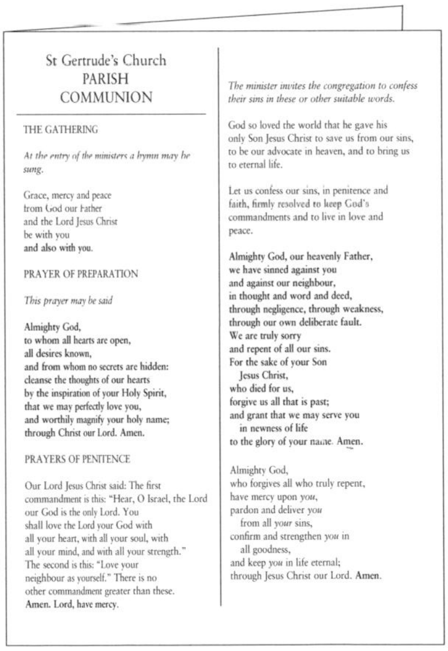

St Gertrude's Church
PARISH
COMMUNION

THE GATHERING

At the entry of the ministers a hymn may be sung.

Grace, mercy and peace
from God our Father
and the Lord Jesus Christ
be with you
and also with you.

PRAYER OF PREPARATION

This prayer may be said

**Almighty God,
to whom all hearts are open,
all desires known,
and from whom no secrets are hidden:
cleanse the thoughts of our hearts
by the inspiration of your Holy Spirit,
that we may perfectly love you,
and worthily magnify your holy name;
through Christ our Lord. Amen.**

PRAYERS OF PENITENCE

Our Lord Jesus Christ said: The first commandment is this: "Hear, O Israel, the Lord our God is the only Lord. You shall love the Lord your God with all your heart, with all your soul, with all your mind, and with all your strength." The second is this: "Love your neighbour as yourself." There is no other commandment greater than these.
Amen. Lord, have mercy.

The minister invites the congregation to confess their sins in these or other suitable words.

God so loved the world that he gave his only Son Jesus Christ to save us from our sins, to be our advocate in heaven, and to bring us to eternal life.

Let us confess our sins, in penitence and faith, firmly resolved to keep God's commandments and to live in love and peace.

**Almighty God, our heavenly Father,
we have sinned against you
and against our neighbour,
in thought and word and deed,
through negligence, through weakness,
through our own deliberate fault.
We are truly sorry
and repent of all our sins.
For the sake of your Son
Jesus Christ,
who died for us,
forgive us all that is past;
and grant that we may serve you
in newness of life
to the glory of your name. Amen.**

Almighty God,
who forgives all who truly repent,
have mercy upon *you*,
pardon and deliver *you*
from all *your* sins,
confirm and strengthen *you* in
all goodness,
and keep *you* in life eternal;
through Jesus Christ our Lord. **Amen.**

Long and thin

Folding an A4 sheet lengthways gives a long thin order of service. It has the advantage of looking and feeling more interesting than the more predictable A5 size.

'Long and thin' also has the advantage of giving a column width which is just about right for the line length of many liturgical texts, which minimizes line breaks and maximizes the use of the paper. With a long and thin orientation you may be able to get most of the service onto one sheet with a font size of 12 point, whereas an A5 format might have needed two columns per page and a reduced font size of 10 point.

For	• Efficient use of space – for single column you can get more on four 'pages' this way than in A5 format. • Most long lines can remain unbroken. • Looks more interesting because of unusual shape. • Some scope for 'white space' on the page. • Fits narrow pew ledges.
Against	• Doesn't work well for multi-sheet booklets. • Not much space for margins, if you need them for instructions like 'Candidate', 'Minister' and so on.
Good for …	• One-off services, or those that are used infrequently, seasonally or annually. • Short services, or formats that don't include all of the leader's text.

St Gertrude's Church
PARISH
COMMUNION

THE GATHERING

At the entry of the ministers a hymn may be sung.

Grace, mercy and peace
from God our Father
and the Lord Jesus Christ
be with you
and also with you.

PRAYER OF PREPARATION

This prayer may be said

Almighty God,
to whom all hearts are open,
all desires known,
and from whom no secrets are hidden:
cleanse the thoughts of our hearts
by the inspiration of your Holy Spirit,
that we may perfectly love you,
and worthily magnify your holy name;
through Christ our Lord. Amen.

PRAYERS OF PENITENCE

Our Lord Jesus Christ said: The first commandment is this: "Hear, O Israel, the Lord our God is the only Lord.
You shall love the Lord your God with all your heart, with all your soul, with all your mind, and with all your strength."
The second is this: "Love your neighbour as yourself." There is no other commandment greater than these.
Amen. Lord, have mercy.

The minister invites the congregation to confess their sins in these or other suitable words.

God so loved the world that he gave his only Son Jesus Christ to save us from our sins, to be our advocate in heaven, and to bring us to eternal life.

A4 landscape threefold

With a threefold leaflet you get more or less the same space for text as an A4 sheet folded lengthways (see page 44), but this time you get it divided into six columns ('pages') rather than four. That may give you the opportunity to make the front page simply a title page with an attractive design, with the text beginning inside the leaflet.

For	• Efficient use of space. • Easy to see the flow of the service (because when opened you can see three columns).
Against	• Some people find threefold leaflets confusing because it is not always clear which section to turn to next. They need clear page numbers.
Good for ...	• One-off services, or those that are used infrequently, seasonally or annually. • Seasonal cards for daily prayer. • Supplementary cards, such as a card with the words of just the baptism, for use in a communion or all-age service that has its own order of service

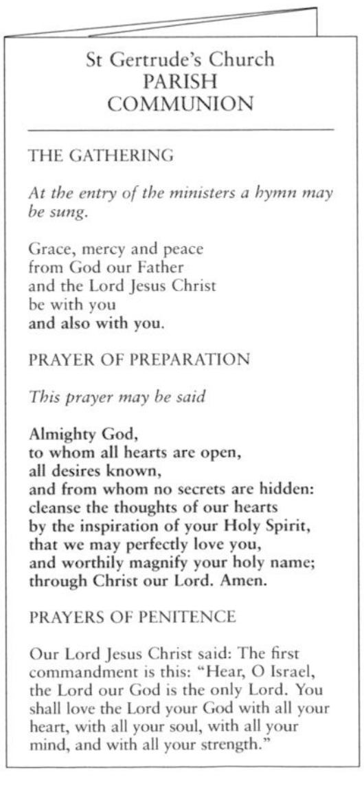

St Gertrude's Church
PARISH
COMMUNION

THE GATHERING

At the entry of the ministers a hymn may be sung.

Grace, mercy and peace
from God our Father
and the Lord Jesus Christ
be with you
and also with you.

PRAYER OF PREPARATION

This prayer may be said

**Almighty God,
to whom all hearts are open,
all desires known,
and from whom no secrets are hidden:
cleanse the thoughts of our hearts
by the inspiration of your Holy Spirit,
that we may perfectly love you,
and worthily magnify your holy name;
through Christ our Lord. Amen.**

PRAYERS OF PENITENCE

Our Lord Jesus Christ said: The first commandment is this: "Hear, O Israel, the Lord our God is the only Lord. You shall love the Lord your God with all your heart, with all your soul, with all your mind, and with all your strength."

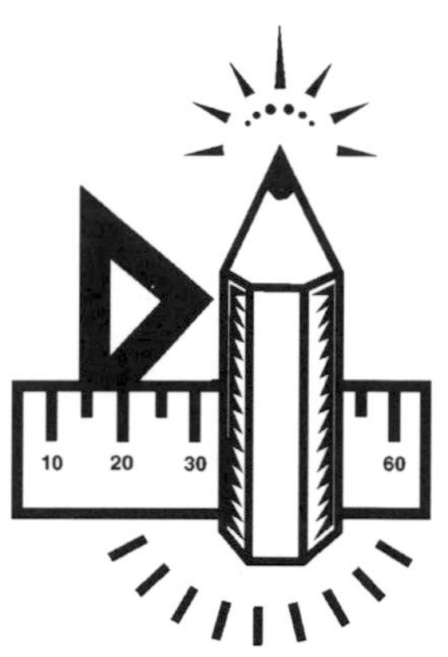

8 Some design principles

The Golden Rule of design

The most important rule of design is that ‘form should follow function’.

Chapter 5 includes some basic liturgical principles which make clear the function of an order of service: it is to enable the worship of the people. Anything that supports that function will be good design. Anything which works against it will not.

Remember above all that the aim is *not* to fit the whole text of this service on as small an amount of paper as possible!

Using white space

When putting a service together we are usually under space constraints, in order to save paper and costs. However, visually the ‘white space’ on the page is just as important as the words and pictures it surrounds. (‘White space’ is a technical term – the paper may be some other colour.) A page of solid text with hardly any space around the words may be an efficient use of paper, but it will be harder to read and not very pleasing to look at. Look at the design of books, and notice how much space there is on the page, and how attractive it is when the margins are generous, and how mean and unattractive it looks when the text goes very close to the edge of the page. The single most important factor in making a liturgical text clear and easy to follow is giving it enough space on the page.

Considering white space will mean taking account of the margins, space between columns of text, font size and style, line spacing, use of pictures and so on.

Choosing a font

Serif fonts

Serif fonts have small projections at the ends of the strokes of the letters, supposedly the remnants of chisel marks made when cutting letters into blocks of stone, and similar to the marks left by the quill pens of medieval times. Serif fonts also tend to have a greater distinction between the thick and thin strokes of the letter.

The theory is that these serifs help to blend letters together horizontally and make it easier for the eye to recognize the shape of the word rather than the individual letters. Serif fonts are therefore particularly good for large blocks of text where it is important for the reader to be able to read easily and quickly.

'Font'

Nothing to do with baptism. Font is another name for a 'typeface', a style of lettering.

Fonts have names like 'Arial' (this font) and 'Times New Roman' (this font).

Serif

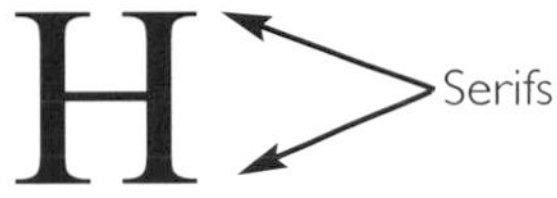

Sans serif fonts

Sans serif (literally, 'without serif') fonts don't have the small projections. These fonts are particularly good at making text clear and distinct. They tend to give a more 'contemporary' feel. They make excellent headings but can also be used for block text – whole books are written in sans serif font, though in theory they would be slightly slower to read than if they were in a serif font. In liturgical texts the line lengths are almost always short so there shouldn't be any loss of readability in using sans serif fonts for the main text.

Sans Serif

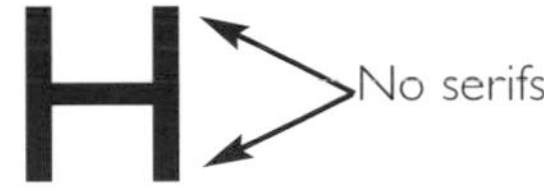

How many fonts

It is a general rule of thumb not to use more than two different fonts in a publication. Each of those fonts may appear in different guises (such as smaller or larger, or bold or italic forms), but there should be no more than two designs of typeface on the page.

Headings, for instance, could be in a different font from the spoken text. Having one sort of font (serif or sans serif) for headings and the other sort for the text often works well. The rubrics could be in a small italic version of the headings or of the main text. The important thing is not to introduce a third font.

No more than **two** fonts in an order of service.

'Points'

The vertical size of print is measured in points. There are 72 points to 1 inch. This text is 10 point.

A simple choice would be to use Arial (sans serif) for headings and rubrics: 14 point bold for headings, and 8 point italic for rubrics. The main text could be Times New Roman 11 point, with bold for the congregation's part. Acknowledgements at the end could be the same as the rubrics, but centre-justified. To introduce a third font would make the service begin to look messy and complicated.

EXAMPLE 1

Headings	Arial, bold, 14 point
Rubrics	Arial, italic, 8 point
Minister's text	Times, 11 point
Congregation's text	Times, 11 point, bold

Here's another, using Frutiger as the main text and Perpetua for headings:

EXAMPLE 2

HEADINGS	Perpetua, bold, 14 point, capitals
Rubrics	Frutiger, italic, 8 point
Minister's text	Frutiger, 11 point
Congregation's text	Frutiger, 11 point, bold

Here's an example using just one font (as the ASB did):

EXAMPLE 3

HEADINGS	Garamond, bold, 14 point, capitals
Rubrics	Garamond, italic, 8 point
Minister's text	Garamond, 11 point
Congregation's text	Garamond, 11 point, bold

Here's one using only sans serif fonts:

EXAMPLE 4

HEADINGS	Gill Sans Condensed, 14 point, capitals
Rubrics	Arial, italic, 8 point
Minister's text	Arial, 11 point
Congregation's text	Arial Black, 11 point

Changing the font rather than the point size can make more or less white space and give larger or smaller looking text, even if the point size remains the same. This is because fonts differ in the way they are shaped, and in particular in the proportion of the font given over to the main part of a letter. Technically this is called the x-height of a font, being the height of a lower case letter 'x'.

If two fonts are both printed in 12 point, the one with the larger x-height will usually look larger, because the main part of the letter will be larger. In the example both paragraphs are in 12 point, but the lower one looks larger. Indeed, the words in the lower paragraph do take up more room horizontally, but not vertically. However, fonts with large x-heights sometimes need a larger line spacing to improve readability.

Same size – different font

Let us confess our sins in penitence and faith, firmly resolved to live in love and peace with all.

(Garamond, 12 point)

Let us confess our sins in penitence and faith, firmly resolved to live in love and peace with all.

(Arial, 12 point)

Headings

You may need two levels of headings: one for the main sections of the service (Gathering, Prayers, Word, Supper) and another for the headings of particular items (Prayers of Intercession, The Peace, The Eucharistic Prayer).

See 'Finding your place' page 58 for discussion about the pros and cons of section numbers.

The first of these will be particularly important for giving a sense of the shape and direction of the service. They could form a running head or footer on every page to which they apply. Or you might have them as a vertical border on every page. A visual icon could also help members of the congregation to orientate themselves. Usually a heading will be placed in the main body of the text, but if you have the luxury of a spacious margin you could experiment.

See Appendix 2, Examples 5 and 6, pages 88–91.

'Sentence case'

Only the first word in the sentence (or heading) has a capital initial letter. The only other capitals would be for proper nouns.

It may be right to use a different font for headings to the one you've used for the main text of the service. A heading is one of the few places where it might be appropriate to use entirely uppercase lettering. However, there is no need to capitalize the first letters of all major words in headings – use normal 'sentence case' text instead (see, for example, the headings in this book). If you use a large and 'heavy' font you may not need to use bold. Headings need space; space before and after a heading helps it to 'breathe' and emphasizes its significance. A good rule of thumb is to keep the space before the heading twice the size of the space after.

Headings normally look neatest if they are aligned to the left with the rest of the text. However, you could experiment and see if a centred heading looks better.

Headings in services should be kept short and sweet. Make sure there are no word breaks in the headings – if necessary go on to an extra line.

A missing heading:

THE BLESSING

Go in peace,
to love and serve the Lord.
In the name of Christ. Amen.

An extra heading is needed:

THE BLESSING

THE DISMISSAL
Go in peace,
to love, etc …

Beware headings that have no text attached ('Sermon', for instance). Make sure that any text that does follow has its own heading to avoid confusion. For instance, in the example on the left, another heading is needed ('The dismissal'?) or a rubric that explains that the blessing is given and then the text following is used.

Develop your own house style

It is essential to have a written house style if there is more than one person involved in the production of orders of service. A house style is simply a list of conventions that you will use in all of your services. It can help to give a sense of identity, coherence and consistency. That might be particularly important if you are producing a lot of service leaflets or cards. Consistency of style and layout will help the congregation to feel at home and you will be less likely to make mistakes or give contradictory instructions.

If you are likely to produce many orders of service it will be well worth taking time to develop your house style. This might be the case if you are producing a new sheet for each monthly all-age service, or personalized orders of service for baptisms, marriages and funerals, or a set of seasonal booklets for parish communion. You may need to take some time experimenting and getting feedback from different people before you decide on a consistent way of doing things.

Sometimes a house style will not apply to everything. For instance, you may want your all-age service leaflet to look different from your main Sunday Eucharist, but a house style will give you a starting point. Even if you end up with several house styles for different sorts of service, some things (such as spelling) will be consistent across them all.

In some circumstances a house style might mean something as simple as deciding which font to use for your services and agreeing always to use bold for the congregation responses. But it might also include guidelines about any or all of the following:

- page definition – size and orientation of paper, size of margins;
- font and size for leader's text;
- font and size for the congregation's text;
- font and size and style (capitals? lower case?) for headings;
- how many levels of headings, their alignment, and how to distinguish the different levels;
- font and size for rubrics and notes;
- whether or not to give numbers to the sections;
- whether or not to use page numbers (and where to put them, what font and size);
- how to refer to your church (e.g. 'St Thomas' Church' or 'The Parish Church of St Thomas the Apostle');
- whether to print directions about posture and, if so, which ones;
- a consistent set of headings and titles;
- spelling conventions (will you 'baptise' or 'baptize'?);
- a standard set of icons or images.

RNIB

The Royal National Institute for the Blind (RNIB) produces a great deal of material about the design of printed text, bearing in mind the needs of those with some form of visual impairment. There is a large amount of material on their web site: www.rnib.org.uk – this includes their 'Clear Print Guidelines'. Alternatively you can get in touch with their Public Policy Department (Tel: 020 7388 1266) for further information or to order any of their publications.

Making it easy to read

All of us benefit from text that is easy to read. For some people, however, ease of reading will make the difference between being able to join in or not.

Basic rules for easy reading

- There is no hard and fast rule about serif or sans serif fonts for ease of reading (see page 47). Though serif fonts are often said to be easier to follow because the shape of the word is clearer, some people with visual impairment find that the clarity of the individual letters in sans serif fonts makes them easier.
- Check the contrast. Black print on white or yellow paper gives the best contrast. Avoid dark shades of paper and pale shades of colour print. Avoid yellow print like the plague.
- Don't run text across a picture or 'watermark'. It looks good, but makes the text harder to read.
- When choosing a font, look for medium or heavy 'weight' (that is, prefer fonts in which the strokes are 'thick' not 'thin').
- Reverse printing (white text on black background, for instance) is okay as long as the typeface is not too light (i.e. 'thin') or too small. However, it often does not reproduce well on photocopiers or duplicators anyway, so is best used sparingly, and never for large amounts of text.
- Keep the type size large. A type size of 10 or 11 point will be adequate for the general reader, but anyone with visual impairment will find it easier if the main text is 12 point, and 14 point is even better if you have the space. It may be possible to have the congregation's part printed in large print and the minister's words smaller.
- If you are planning a large print version of your order of service, aim for a type size of 14 or 16 point.
- Avoid 'bizarre' typefaces. (You may be able to get away with sparing use of more unusual fonts for headings, but not for text.)
- Keep text aligned to the left and leave right hand margins unjustified, or 'ragged' (like this text).

- Leave reasonable space between lines. Don't be tempted to close up the line spacing to fit something onto the paper.
- Try to avoid very long lines of text.
- If you are using double columns of text, make sure that the gap between is large enough to make the two columns distinct, or use a vertical line to separate them.
- Don't use shiny paper – it reflects too much light and makes it hard to read the print.

Making an impression

As well as the obvious implications for legibility mentioned above, your choice of font will also give your order of service a certain 'feel'. You can make a service look classic, safe, informal, contemporary, unusual, young, welcoming, staid, forbidding, complicated ... and so on, all by the use of different fonts and other design techniques.

Bizarre or informal fonts are fun, and may be appropriate for some services. Sometimes the use of an unusual font can stimulate and challenge assumptions, but there is also the potential to distract from the worship itself and even to give offence. For instance, most people would find the use of a font such as 'Flora Medium' inappropriately informal for a funeral service. However, it is possible that for the funeral of a child it might be suitable, as long as it was a decision shared by the family. For an all-age service it could be just right for the informal feel you might want to give. The important thing is to be aware of the impact of the font *before* you print 100 copies of the order of service!

Compare the effect of the font on the 'feel' of this prayer:

Almighty God,
to whom all hearts are open,
all desires known,
and from whom no secrets are
hidden:
cleanse the thoughts of our hearts
by the inspiration of your
Holy Spirit,
that we may perfectly love you,
and worthily magnify your
holy name;
through Christ our Lord. Amen.
(Times New Roman)

*Almighty God,
to whom all hearts are open,
all desires known,
and from whom no secrets
are hidden:
cleanse the thoughts of
our hearts
by the inspiration of your
Holy Spirit,
that we may perfectly love you,
and worthily magnify you
holy name;
through Christ our Lord. Amen.
(Flora Medium)*

Using pictures

Pictures can liven up any order of service and a well-chosen illustration can also help to interpret what is going on in the service. They can serve both as decoration and as a visual signpost. Small pictures can serve as visual 'icons' (in the computer sense of the word), indicating posture, singing, different elements of the service and so on. There is a wealth of clip art around, Christian and secular, and usually there is something to suit.

Here are some basic guidelines:

- Less is more with clip art – don't overdo it.
- Try to keep to a consistent, or at least complementary, style within any one publication.
- Remember that a distracting, poor or inappropriate picture is worse than no picture.
- Try to avoid giving offence. Ask one or two other people to look at your final order of service and to comment on the pictures as well as the text.
- Try to avoid gender and other forms of stereotyping in your illustrations (be especially careful in selecting pictures for a 'family' or all age service) and look for an appropriate racial mix in the pictures you use over a period of time.

Using colour

Using colour copying for locally produced orders of service is likely to be out of the price range of most churches (in the near future, anyway).

However, for a special service (such as a wedding, or possibly a baptism) it is possible to add a little colour at reasonable cost for small print runs. The way to do it is to print the main service using the usual technology in black and white. Then run those pre-printed service orders through a colour inkjet printer attached to your computer to add a small area of colour (perhaps a photo, a picture, or some coloured lines). Obviously the alignment of the colour on the pre-printed sheets is crucial and the technique is both time consuming and would be costly if done in large numbers. But once in a while it might just be worth it …

Another way of adding areas of colour is to go to your local printer and ask them to produce large quantities of a basic sheet, which you could use for all your services, or all the covers of your booklets. It would work like a standard letterhead. It might include the name of your church and perhaps a picture of it. You would then print the text of the different services in black and white using your normal technology.

Tips for printing liturgical texts

Bold for congregational texts

This means that you don't have to print 'Minister' and 'All' in the left-hand margin. It makes the text look less cluttered and if space is tight (as it almost always is) it means that you can make the columns narrower, and perhaps put two columns on a page. However, make sure that the bold is really bold and easily distinguished from the normal text. An alternative is to use *italic*, though italic is often used for rubrics and instructions.

Like this:

The Lord be with you.
And also with you.

Never use upper case lettering for congregational text

When we fill in forms we are always asked to use capitals and so most of us instinctively feel that capitals are clear and easy to read. In fact they are not, because it is impossible to discern the word from its shape. This is something we all do subconsciously and it makes us able to read more easily and quickly. For people whose vision is impaired it is doubly important. Using capitals is also difficult for children, who usually learn capitals after they have learned lower case letters.

The other problem with using upper case is that it makes it look as if the words are to be shouted – so save capitals for when you *do* want them to be shouted.

Upper case lettering is usually acceptable for headings.

Not like this:

The Lord be with you
AND ALSO WITH YOU.

Make rubrics distinctive

Rubrics and instructions that are not part of the spoken text should be indicated by using a different typeface, or by using *italic*. It is usually clearer if rubrics and instructions are in a smaller size than spoken texts (8 or 9 point would be typical). It is best to keep a small line space between rubrics and the text that follows them.

This response may be used:

Lord in your mercy,
hear our prayer.

Lining out prayers

Our Father which art in heaven, Hallowed be thy Name. Thy kingdom come. Thy will be done, in earth as it is in heaven.
(BCP)

becomes:

Our Father,
which art in heaven,
hallowed be thy Name;
thy kingdom come;
thy will be done;
in earth as it is in heaven.

Turn-overs

not:

as we forgive those who sin against
us.

but:

as we forgive those
  who sin against us.

'Line out' prayers said by the congregation

'Lining out' is the process of breaking prayers down into short lines that help to make sense of the prayer (hence they are often called 'sense lines'). They also make it easier for the congregation to keep together and to know when to pause for breath (hence they are also sometimes called 'speech-equivalent lines').

In *The Book of Common Prayer* the words said by the congregation were printed in big blocks of print, split into short sections by the use of capital letters. In recent years it has become the norm instead to break congregational texts into separate lines. Note that the capital letters have also dropped out at the start of lines, unless it is the start of a new sentence. This makes it easier to read and makes the sense clearer. Many of us were taught at school that for poetry we should use a capital letter at the start of every line, whether it began a new sentence or not, and that is a hard lesson to unlearn!

Where a line is too long to fit the column width, the continuation (or 'turn-over') should be indented rather than lined up with the left margin. This makes it clearer that it is a continuation of the line above (and is therefore a visible warning not to take a breath at that point). Care is needed to make sure that the turn-over comes at a sensible point in the sentence (in terms of its sense) and doesn't leave a single word all on its own on the continuation line.

Note that text for the leader does not necessarily need to be lined out in this way. Because the leader is speaking alone, he or she does not need the visual clues that help to keep a congregation speaking together. He or she should also be familiar with the *sense* of the words and not need short lines for that reason. This can also help to distinguish between the words said by the leader and those said by the congregation.

Justification

For liturgical text there is no need to 'justify' the text (giving neat edges to left and right margins of a block of text). Most lines will be short anyway and where there is a large block of text (such as minister's text) it is not necessary to justify it. Justifying text in fairly narrow columns usually results in lots of hyphens or lots of large spaces between words – neither of which looks very professional. Stick to an 'align left'/'ragged right' setting.

Avoid 'centred' text (with both left and right margins 'ragged') – it is harder to find the beginning of the next line.

Justification

To make your text as easy as possible to read, stick to an 'align-left'/'ragged right' setting, like this text.

Don't be tempted to justify text like this (with left and right edges neatly aligned) – it looks neat but it is harder to read. The word spacing becomes irregular and the eye finds it harder to tell what line you are on.

And centred text, like this, is
also not easy to read, because
the eye can't find the beginning
of the line so easily.

'Cue lines' to lead the congregation in

A way of avoiding introductions like 'We say together ...' is to print cue lines before congregational texts. This is particularly useful when a congregational text follows a silence and the congregation has no way of knowing when to start. For instance, after the eucharistic prayer the Lord's Prayer needs some sort of introductory cue line. The *Common Worship* services suggest different cue lines depending on which version of the Lord's Prayer is used.

A similar technique can be used in other situations, particularly where you have a choice of texts, but both start with the same words (for instance, two confessions which both begin, 'Almighty God ...').

For the modern Lord's Prayer use:

As our Saviour taught us, so we pray

For the modified traditional form use:

Let us pray with confidence as our Saviour has taught us

Capitals

We have already seen that using upper case lettering makes reading harder and so does the unnecessary use of capitals at the start of words and lines.

Words with unnecessary capital first letters also interrupt the visual flow of a line. Pronouns for God (You, Your, Thee, Thine, His, Him, etc.) are not capitalized in modern Bible translations, and there is no need to capitalize them in liturgical texts, unless it is necessary to make the meaning clear (for instance, if it is not clear to whom the 'him' refers).

Compare:

hallowed be Thy Name;

with:

hallowed be thy name;

Take care with page breaks

Make sure that congregational text (such as a confession) is not broken by a page turn; a column break, or a break between the bottom of a left-hand page and the top of a right-hand page is not so bad. If you really must have a page break in a congregational text (perhaps for a one-off service where space is at an absolute premium) then make sure that the break comes at a sensible place – not mid-sentence, for instance. Better still, think again about the design, page layout and so on. In addition, page breaks should not separate a heading from the text to which it refers, nor a rubric from the text which follows it.

Printing songs and hymns

Sometimes an order of service will also include the full text of hymns or songs. Though they are congregational text it usually looks odd to print them in bold. If you have used only one font for the rest of the text and headings it may be appropriate to use a different font for songs and hymns.

The complications really come when parts of the liturgy are sung. It is worth thinking about how to signal this by the typeface or rubrics.

Finding your place

See also the discussion under 'Headings', above. See Appendix 2, Examples 4, 5 and 6 (pages 86–91) for different approaches.

In any order of service it will be important to make sure that you can direct the congregation to the right place. Even if you wish to keep announcements to a minimum in a normal service, there will be times when something special will interrupt the flow of the service (perhaps something extra, or something omitted) and you will need to tell the congregation where the service continues.

A fairly basic requirement will be for the headings to be clearly distinguished from the main text and large enough to be found easily on the page.

There are no hard and fast rules about section numbers and headings. They can provide an easy way to direct people to the right place, but can sound a bit mechanical when announced. What's more, they can look ugly, and need distinguishing from the text of a heading. Otherwise you risk

'10 Prayers of intercession'.

The best way, if possible, is to put any section numbers in the left margin, and make them smaller than the heading itself.

If you are not going to use section numbers, make sure you have thought about what you will do. Will headings be enough? Will they end up being more confusing than section numbers ('We turn to the bottom of the second column of page 3 where the heading says ...')? All but the simplest service cards will probably need page numbers. Where will you put them (they don't have to go at the bottom)? How large will you make them? How will you keep them from getting confused with the text of the service?

Images can also help the congregation to find the place. When visitors lose the place in the service, they will look around to see if they can work out which page everyone else is on. If they can see a picture on the page it will make it easier for them to find their place.

A design check-list

- Check how many fonts you have used. Do they work together?
- Check that the text (especially the congregational text) is aligned left/ragged right.
- Check that long lines break or turn-over at sensible places.
- Check page breaks. Make sure you haven't split a congregational text across a page turn.
- Check that you have indicated which texts (if any) are to be sung.
- Have you thought about how people will find their place (including consideration of headings, section numbers and page numbers)?
- Are the margins wide enough, and is there enough white space on each page?
- Is the line spacing sufficient?
- Are the headings clear, but not dominant?
- Check for hyphens and remove them.
- Could the print size be larger, without spoiling other aspects of the design?
- Would a different font be clearer?
- Is the 'look and feel' of the order of service appropriate to its purpose?
- Are there enough pictures? Are they appropriate and in the right places?
- Have you included all necessary rubrics? Are there unnecessary rubrics you could remove? Are the rubrics in the right places?

9 Practical matters

Equipment

New technology has made it possible to do new things and to do old things better. But it doesn't stop the old technology from working. The sort of quality we are used to from desktop publishing can lure us into thinking that nothing less will do – but sometimes something less *will* do. So, before you launch out on expensive new equipment or spend long hours slaving over the computer getting every last detail perfect, ask yourself, 'What is the "good enough" solution to this need?' It may be that scissors and paste will give a good enough result this time and may save you several hours too. On the whole, the skill and knowledge of the operator will have a much greater impact on the final product than the available technology.

Computer

A computer is not strictly speaking necessary. A good typewriter or non-computer word processor could produce readable text, or you could use a photocopier and good old-fashioned scissors and paste – and before the advent of home computers, that's what most people did if they wanted to produce their own orders of service. Alternatively, they went to a professional printer who did the job for them.

However, doing the work yourself on your own computer (or working with those among your congregation who have the technology) has several advantages:

- It is much more flexible and considerably cheaper than using a printing company. That makes it much easier to make changes and to produce orders of service for different occasions without breaking the bank.

- Modern word processing and desktop publishing programs (coupled with a good printer – see pages 63–64) can give much more flexible and professional looking results than a typewriter. These days people *expect* to see that sort of 'professional look' on everything from meeting agendas to school newsletters. Anything typewritten can look very dated and dull in comparison.
- You can store your services electronically and use one as the basis for different variants. For instance, your basic order for Holy Communion can become the basis for special orders for Lent or Advent, and you don't have to start from scratch.
- You can take advantage of liturgy on the Internet or computer disk and you can use software such as *Visual Liturgy* to help you and to save on typing (see Chapter 4).
- You can easily try out different designs and styles to see which is easiest to use and most attractive.

Appropriate software

This may include something like the *Visual Liturgy* worship planning software, but it will certainly include a decent word processor and may include a basic desktop publishing (DTP) program.

The main advantage of DTP software is that it makes it easier to print multi-page booklets with the pages in the right order for copying. Some word processors also include this feature.

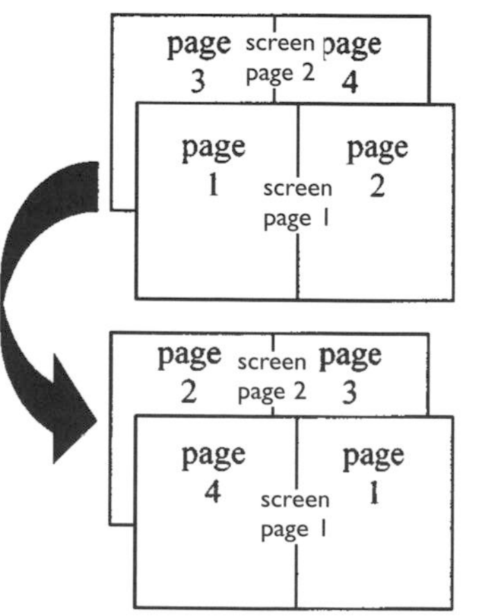

If you don't have any software that does this, then it is fairly easy to achieve the same result for a four-page leaflet, either using cut and paste on a word processor or on real paper.

Using a word processor

Set up the document with two columns (each column represents a printed page) and produce the text on two screen pages. When it is in its final form, cut the text from page 4 and paste it in at the beginning of page 1. The text flows automatically, all the pages move one column further on and all is ready for photocopying back to back with no hand cutting and pasting.

Using paper

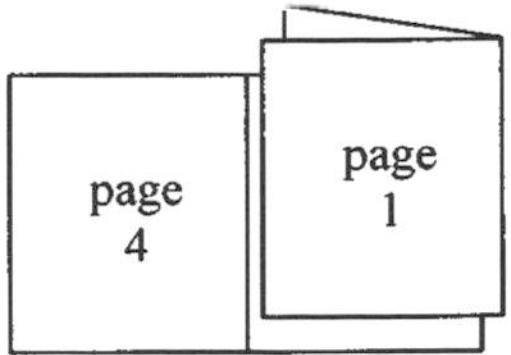

Print all four 'pages' on the left-hand sides of separate sheets of A4 paper, in landscape (horizontal) orientation (set the right-hand margin to exclude text from the right-hand side of the pages). Fold the odd numbered pages in half and tuck them round the blank right-hand side of the even numbered pages.

A good quality original

A good quality order of service depends chiefly on producing a high quality original. For computer users that will mean a decent printer.

Laser and inkjet printers

Either of these should be capable of producing excellent quality originals. Set the quality to its best setting – the highest number of 'dots per inch' (dpi).

If you are using an inkjet printer remember that the quality is affected by the paper as well as by the printer settings. For originals it is worth investing in some of the special coated paper that prevents the ink spreading and 'bleeding'. Ask your stationer for help if you are not sure, or consult your printer manual.

Even a laser printer's output will benefit from good quality paper, but special coatings are not necessary.

Dot matrix printers

The quality is not as good as laser or inkjet printers; it will depend on the number of pins in the print head. A 24-pin printer will produce the best results, but the dots are still visible to the naked eye and the contrast tends not to be so good (it's hard to get a really solid black). However, the results may be good enough for your purposes. Dot matrix printers are not always able to handle large fonts and they won't be able to deal well with clip art, illustrations or other decoration.

Daisy wheel printers

These can give clear print but are not as versatile as the others, as the type size and style is limited to what is available on the daisy wheel. To get different fonts or different sizes the print head has to be changed. They generally cannot produce the large fonts needed for those with visual impairment.

The same points apply to typewriters.

Producing multiple copies

Photocopier

The photocopier is the obvious choice for most churches and a good one can easily produce the required quality. For large quantities, one that can handle copying on both sides of the paper is a bonus.

Photocopying can be an expensive way of producing local editions if you are going to produce lots of booklets with multiple pages for a large congregation.

Scan duplicator

Scan duplicators (or 'digital wet ink copiers') combine the quality and ease of use of a photocopier with the economy of the old 'Gestetner-type' duplicators – or at least, that's the theory.

They work by scanning the original and recording it in digital form. They use that digital information to make a master copy on a special film, from which all the other copies are printed using a liquid ink. Because they work with the information digitally, it is possible to buy attachments that allow you to feed the information directly from your computer into the copier, without printing out an original. This improves the quality slightly.

This is very fast (faster than photocopying) and very cheap (typically less than a penny a copy) and is ideal for large print runs where quality does not have to be absolutely perfect. The results are good, but not usually as sharp as a photocopy, and shades of grey don't always come out well. By swapping the ink you can also print in more than one colour. You have to run the copies through twice: once to print the black, then a second time (after changing the ink drum and making a new master) to print the second colour. Clearly, the alignment of the paper on the second pass through the machine is crucial, and not always as accurate as necessary.

Scan duplicators are not designed to replace photocopiers and they are not convenient to use for small numbers of copies. At quantities less than 25 or so they become less economical because of the cost of the film.

They are well worth investigating for churches that produce large numbers of copies regularly. For most church purposes the quality is good enough.

Digital photocopier

The latest innovation in photocopying is the digital photocopier. This combines the technology of the computer scanner with that of the laser printer. The original is scanned and recorded digitally, and the copies are then produced using laser printer technology. Because the original is scanned only once (not for every copy, as with analogue photocopiers) the speed of copying is increased and wear and tear reduced. They are very versatile and usually handle collating, sorting, double-sided copying and booklet formatting with ease. In addition, you can hook up your computer to the copier and use it like a printer.

Copy shop

If your photocopier isn't up to producing the required quality and you can't afford a digital copier, you can always take your originals to a copy shop. The price will be higher, but you save yourself a lot of hard work and the quality should be excellent. If you think you will be a regular customer, try negotiating for a special deal.

Right way up

Most photocopier paper has a 'best side', which is very slightly smoother than the other side. On the end of the packet in which photocopier paper arrives (if you buy in reams – 500-sheet packets) you should find an arrow. The arrow indicates the best side. Paper should be fed into the machine so that this best side is the side printed on. Whether that means loading paper with the best side facing up or down depends on your particular copier. Consult your copier's instruction manual. If you are printing on both sides of the paper, feed it so that the best side is printed on first.

Paper

Colour of paper

Using coloured paper has many advantages:

- It makes an order of service look more special.
- It stands out from other items such as notice sheets or welcome cards.
- It is easier to refer to ('on the yellow card').
- It can reinforce a sense of the church's year (green for ordinary, red for Pentecost and so on).

The main danger is using paper that has a particularly intense or deep colour against which the black print (or other colour print) does not show up clearly. On the whole pastel shades are safer than the more vibrant tones, though any coloured paper (with the possible exception of yellow) will reduce the contrast between print and paper, which may be a problem for those with impaired vision.

If you are producing a booklet it is possible to get the advantages of colour without too many of the problems by printing the cover on coloured card or paper and the inside pages on white.

Weight of paper

Weight of paper is something that can also make a difference to the price and quality of the finished product. Standard photocopier paper is 80 grams per square metre ('gsm' or 'g/m^2'). The greater the weight of paper (i.e. the thicker it is) the more of a 'quality' feel your order of service will have, but the more it will cost.

For a wedding or a funeral, a thicker paper may give the impression that care has been taken over the production of the order of service. A 100 gsm paper feels appreciably thicker and nicer than 80 gsm, but at a price. Much beyond that and you are in the realm of thin card rather than thick paper.

If you are producing a booklet, you may want to use a thin card for the outer cover, and standard 80 gsm paper for the inner pages. A heavier paper will make a simple single folded sheet order of service easier to handle and more durable.

Thicker paper may also be necessary if you are using a scan duplicator ('wet ink' digital copier). Sometimes the ink can show through to the other side of the paper if the paper is not thick enough. Do a test before you print the whole lot. Note also that smooth paper can result in ink transferring from one piece of paper to another as the sheets land on one another after printing.

Don't forget that paper thickness may limit your printing options. Not all copiers can handle thick paper or card (for instance, if the paper feed requires the paper to be contorted this way and that to move from the paper tray to the copier mechanism). Some copiers that do handle card require you to feed every sheet manually. It's worth checking before you order the paper.

For a really long-lasting card, you can always laminate, but if you are folding the card it can become annoyingly 'springy'. A laminated card can be particularly good at baptisms, where service sheets can get wet (!) and seem especially prone to being chewed by the babies among the guests.

Binding

A folded card is straightforward, but if you are considering a multi-page booklet then you will need to consider the method of binding:

- Staple – works fine for a small number of pages and is both cheap and simple.
- Plastic comb binding – can be good for a thicker booklet (perhaps with songs as well as services). You will need a special machine to do the punching and binding (or you could ask your local printer to do it), but it allows you to update the publication if necessary and the booklet will lie flat when open.

- Plastic slide binding – uses a slip-on plastic spine to hold the sheets together. This can work well for small booklets, but it doesn't allow the booklet to open easily and the plastic spine can slip off as easily as it slipped on. This may be an advantage if you want to update the contents regularly.

Corrections

Keep a copy of each booklet, leaflet or card you produce and write on it all the corrections, comments and emendations that emerge from use. Remember to refer to it if and when you reprint and when you next come to produce an order of service.

If more than one person is responsible for producing orders of service, make sure the corrected copies are kept on file somewhere centrally where everyone has access to them, otherwise you lose some of the opportunity to learn by trial and error.

Losing copies

If you've made a really good job of your order of service people will want to take a copy home. Regulars may want to have one on the shelf and may even use it in their personal prayers. Visitors may want to take one home 'to show their vicar'. Baptism or wedding guests may want to take one home as a reminder of a special occasion for them.

If you've spent a lot of money and time on these orders of service you may therefore want to print a message somewhere in large type asking people not to take the orders of service away with them. Even with a detail like this, take care how you phrase it.

Of course, it may be preferable to take a more positive approach and make sure you print enough so that it doesn't matter if people take them away. There may be cost implications if you have produced booklets with laminated card covers, but a solution may be to invite people (visitors and regulars) to make a donation to cover costs if they wish

Avoiding losing your orders of service

'Not to be removed'
This is clear, but sounds a bit harsh.

'Please do not take away'
This is gentler, but still fairly firm.

'Please return this booklet after the service for future use'
This sounds friendlier, is more positive and explains *why* you want the booklet back. But it may not be obvious to visitors *where* to return the booklet (back of church, end of row, to the stewards, etc.).

to take a copy home. Or you could produce a cheaper version for 'take-aways'.

Sometimes you will actively encourage people to take copies home (for instance, personalized orders of service for a wedding, baptism, thanksgiving or funeral). The *Common Worship* funeral and marriage services include an introduction to the service, intended to be read by the congregation before the service starts. Printing these in orders of service designed to be taken away is a small way of getting some basic Christian teaching into the homes of occasional worshippers.

10 A proof-reading check-list

- Run the spellcheck one more time (assuming you are using a computer). I know you've done it a dozen times already, but that last minute change you made is bound to have included a spelling mistake that you missed in your rush.
- Check that the spellcheck is not set to *American* English.
- Read through the whole service carefully when you are not under pressure. The spellcheck will not pick up every spelling problem in liturgical text. For instance, 'Left up your hearts', seems as sensible to the spellcheck as, 'Lift up your hearts'.
- Go back and check your text against the published service for incidental errors, including unintended variations in spelling, punctuation and use of capitals.
- Get someone else to read through the whole service. They will be more likely to spot typing errors that have slipped through the net. Good people to ask are those annoying folk who always come up to you after the service to point out this week's typos and errors in the notice sheet.
- Get some people to read through the service and check for things that are unclear or ambiguous.
- Check the rubrics – have you included all the posture instructions that you intended to?
- Check for *consistency* of spelling (e.g. have you put 'baptise' in one place and 'baptize' in another?). Even your spellcheck may allow such inconsistency.
- Check line breaks and turn-overs again – are they still in sensible places?
- Check page breaks again – avoid splitting congregational texts across two pages.

- Check for hyphens at the end of lines. Most, if not all, should be avoided. Make sure that auto-hyphenation is turned off.
- Check headings – especially long ones that go onto a second line.
- Check the bottom of pages and columns for single lines left on their own, or for headings or rubrics separated from the text to which they refer.
- Check for uneven line spacing. This is sometimes caused during editing when an invisible character (such as a space) set in a larger point-size sneaks its way into your text.
- Check for missing line spaces. This sometimes happens when a page break moves during editing. You may have cut out a line space between the end of one item and the heading for the next because it left a space at the top of a page. If you subsequently cut some other text at the beginning of the service, that missing line space moves to the middle of a page.
- To check other mysterious effects, set your software to display formatting characters such as spaces, tabs and returns (see your manual or onscreen Help for details). All may be revealed!
- Check printing – has your printer cut off the first letters or last letters of sentences on the left or right margins?
- Check bold print – has congregational text (and only congregational text) come out in bold every time it should?

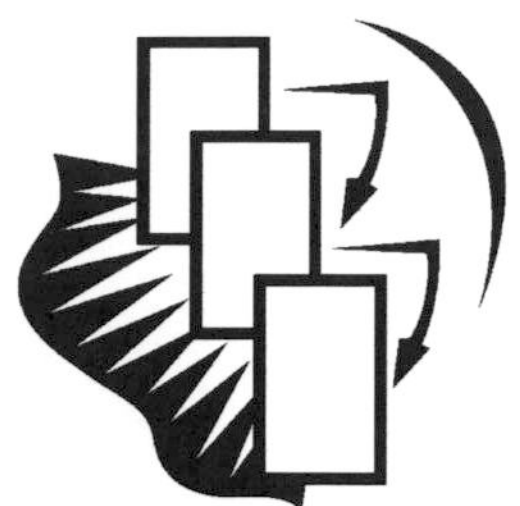

11 Flowchart

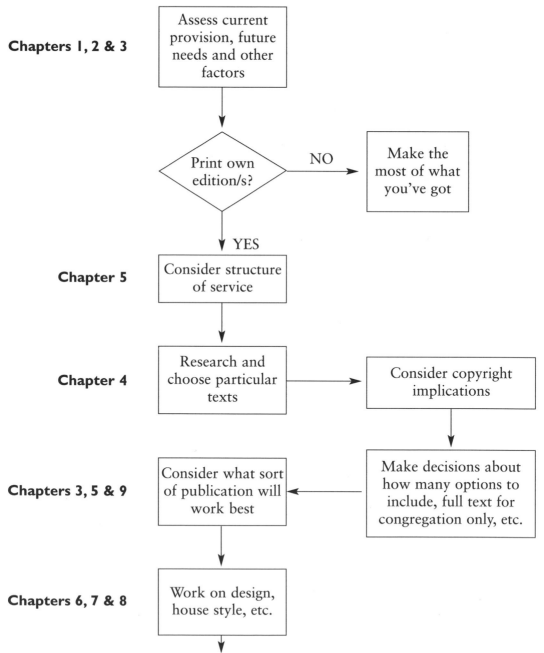

Chapters 1, 2 & 3	Assess current provision, future needs and other factors		
	↓		
	Print own edition/s?	NO →	Make the most of what you've got
	↓ YES		
Chapter 5	Consider structure of service		
	↓		
Chapter 4	Research and choose particular texts	→	Consider copyright implications
			↓
Chapters 3, 5 & 9	Consider what sort of publication will work best	←	Make decisions about how many options to include, full text for congregation only, etc.
	↓		
Chapters 6, 7 & 8	Work on design, house style, etc.		
	↓		

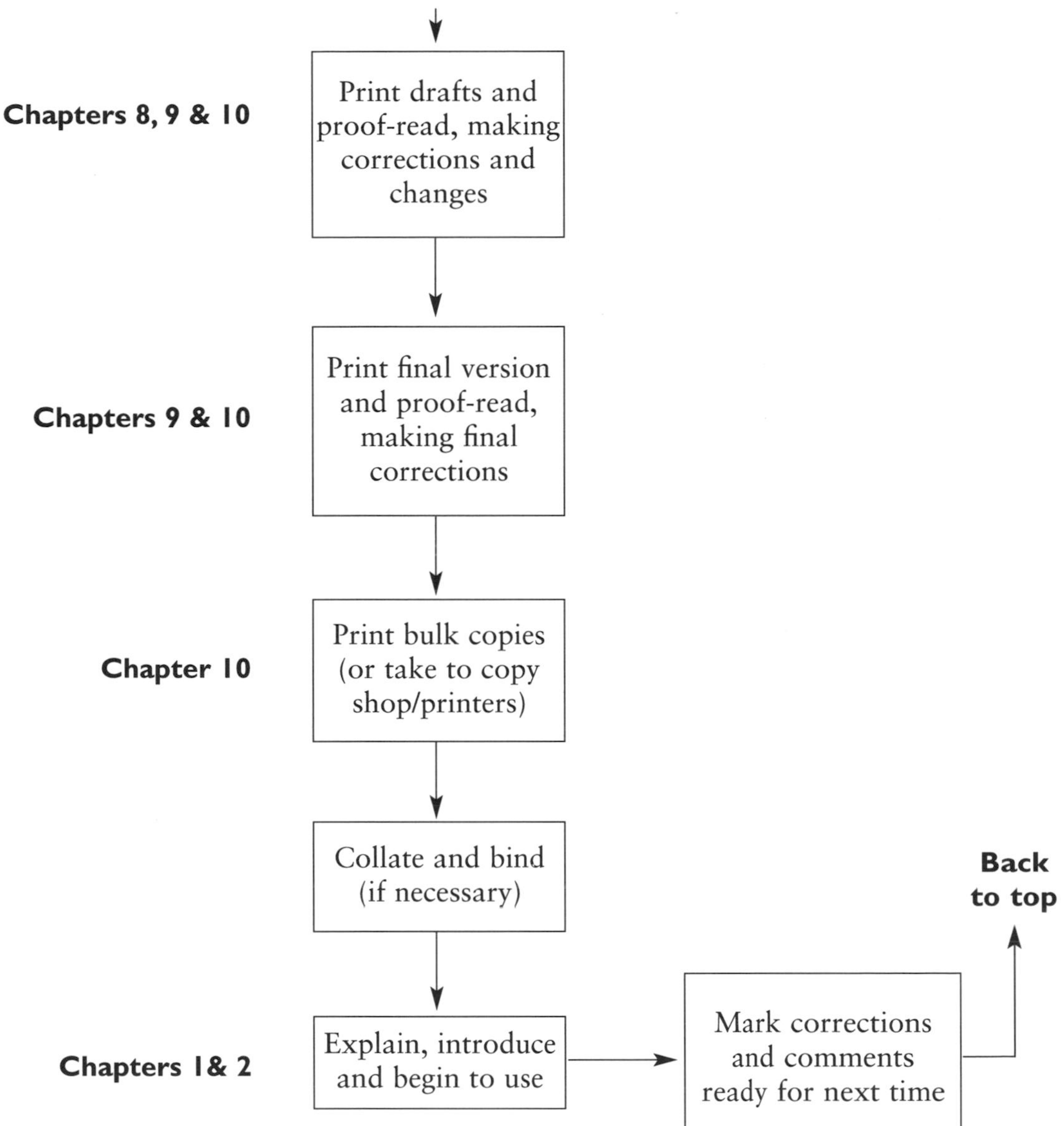

Chapters 8, 9 & 10
Print drafts and proof-read, making corrections and changes
Chapters 9 & 10
Print final version and proof-read, making final corrections
Chapter 10
Print bulk copies (or take to copy shop/printers)
Collate and bind (if necessary)
Chapters 1& 2
Explain, introduce and begin to use
Mark corrections and comments ready for next time
Back to top

Appendix 1
Using an overhead projector

Many churches already use an overhead projector (OHP) and more and more have a data projector driven directly from a computer for the words of songs, but both can also be used successfully for the projection of spoken texts. There are several advantages over books, booklets and printed sheets:

- People are looking up, rather than down at a book, and this makes it easier to maintain a sense of corporate worship rather than individual recitation of texts.
- It is therefore easier to maintain a focus for the service, as people can see what is happening at the same time as reading texts.
- It is easier to make last-minute changes to the order of service because the congregation do not have detailed orders of service from which you are departing. You can also have a large amount of liturgical material available from which you can select as appropriate during the service.
- The service can flow more easily, as people do not have to turn from a hymnbook to an order of service. A full printed order of service, including hymns, can achieve the same thing, but using a projector is more flexible and allows for changes, even at the last minute. For most churches a detailed printed order of service for each Sunday is unrealistic, and is reserved for special services, such as Christmas carol services.
- You can include new material or replace material at the last minute because all that is needed is the production of one slide, rather than the printing of a large number of sheets.

- You can include material that is not in the books or orders of service that the congregation is using. Hence it is possible to use a basic order of service, perhaps on paper and on screen, yet vary it from week to week using additional or different material on screen.
- The members of the congregation don't need to hold anything and so are free to clap or do other demonstrative things with their hands (if this is desirable!).

The negative aspects are:

- The congregation may have no idea what is coming next. At one end of the scale this means that they don't know what the next part of the eucharistic prayer is going to contain and what their part will be. At the other end of the scale, they don't see what structural element is coming next (for instance, what will follow the eucharistic prayer). Some churches work on this principle all the time (!) but in a liturgical tradition it is more normal for the congregation to have some idea of what is to follow.
- Many people find it hard to see the words on a screen. This may be because of visual impairment, because the sun is shining on the screen, or because the building is large or is shaped so that many people cannot easily see a screen. It is possible to use more than one screen, but you risk losing both focus and a sense of corporate worship, as people are looking in different directions.
- For some parts of a service it feels more natural to be looking down, rather than up at a screen – confession, for example.
- Some people simply have a gut feeling that there is something inherently inappropriate about using an OHP for worship.

You can overcome some of the problems and gain some of the benefits by trying as far as possible to provide items both in print and on screen so that worshippers can choose which to use. There may still be some items that only appear on the screen, but at least the *whole* service will not be a blur to someone who cannot see it.

Preparing liturgical texts for projection

Most of the standard advice given in other sections about the presentation of liturgical texts applies here also, but there are some issues that are particular to the use of an OHP or data projector.

Use a big enough font

It is tempting simply to use something that you already have on paper and photocopy it onto acetate. OHPs need a much bigger font. Try not to use anything smaller than 30 point.

Text for OHP needs to be about this size (30 point).

Use bold which is really bold

This applies to texts printed on paper too, but some fonts that work on paper don't work on OHP – the bold is not clearly bolder, and the result is that everyone says all the words, including the leader's text. This is a particular danger if you are using a photocopier to enlarge text onto OHP acetate – by the time the text has been printed on paper, enlarged and printed onto the acetate, it may not be at all clear which text is bold and which isn't.

Some suggested fonts:

- Abadi
- Lucida
- Arial (you get an even clearer distinction if you use Arial Black for the bold print, not just the bold version of Arial)

Another way of making congregational text clear on OHP is to indent congregational text slightly, so that it can be distinguished from the leader's text. This can be a bit limiting for long texts such as creeds or prayers (because it effectively increases the left margin and wastes space) but it can work well for sets of responses.

Congregational text can also be printed in a larger font than the leader's text.

The Lord be with you.
And also with you.
(Abadi)

The Lord be with you.
And also with you.
(Lucida)

The Lord be with you.
(Arial)
And also with you.
(Arial Black)

The Lord be with you.
(Arial)
And also with you.
(Arial bold)

Change the slides in sensible places

If you have a creed on OHP, it is no good if the slide has to be changed in the middle of a sentence:

> **and we believe in** *[change slide]*
>
> **the Holy Spirit.**

Not only does it break the sense of the sentence by having an induced pause in the middle, it also breaks the rhythm, so that when the next slide is ready people will not be synchronized.

Show the structure of the service

On paper people can get a glimpse of the overall shape of the service before it even starts, even if the sheet does not print every word of text. This is more difficult with words on a screen. One solution is to display a diagram of the key elements of the service discreetly before you start so that people have an idea of the ground to be covered. Another option (which can be used with or without the structure diagram) is to use a colour code or running title to indicate which section of the service you are in. You could use simple terms like, 'Gathering', 'Word', 'Prayer' and so on to make clear what is happening in each part of the service.

If you use OHP with paper (a notice sheet, perhaps, or an outline order of service) you can use it to give the overall shape and the screen to give particular texts.

Using an OHP in worship

Positioning the equipment

An OHP screen needs to be visible but it should not obscure any first order visual focus for worship such as the holy table, font, lectern or symbols such as banners or crosses. It should not appear to the casual visitor that we worship an overhead projector. Nevertheless the screen must not be too far from the visual focus. If the screen is too far to one side the congregation's attention will be divided. As a general rule the screen and the worship leader should not be too far apart, so that people can see both screen and leader without looking in two different directions. If the leader is also operating the OHP then it becomes doubly important that leader, screen and OHP are all fairly close.

Brief the operator well

Operating an OHP for spoken texts is a different skill to using it for songs. For songs, there are extra aural clues as to what is going on. Often people will recognize the song from the musical introduction, and a choir or music group will give a clear lead, so that if the words of the song are a few seconds late, the congregation can usually busk the first few lines if they need to.

With liturgical texts it is not so clear, and so the words need to appear a couple of seconds *before* they are needed, not after. The minister should not need to say, 'Now we will confess our sins, using the words *that should appear on the screen in a moment*.'

Used well, an OHP can enable the service to flow with a minimum of announcements, even if many in the congregation are visitors or the service contains a lot of material which is new.

Handling breaks

Between liturgical items make sure the OHP is turned off (or the light is blocked in some way).

Alternatively, use a standard 'blank screen'. This might be something like a cross or some other symbol. This can be particularly useful when using a data projector rather than an OHP with acetates.

Appendix 2
Examples

The examples that follow are all based on real orders of service from real churches, though most have been altered slightly to suit the present purpose. For the sake of simplicity and ease of comparison of different approaches they have all been portrayed in A5 format, but most could just as easily be used in other ways.

They are not included here as examples of perfection, nor is the choice of text or the wording of headings intended as a blueprint to be followed by others. However, in general (with the notable exception of Example 2) they illustrate good practice, in the sense of 'practice that would be good in the right circumstances', not in the sense of 'the right answer for every situation'. They are simply included to show some of the possibilities and to illustrate some of the points made elsewhere in the book.

Example 1

This very simple example is clear and easy to follow.

The text and rubrics are all the same large, clear 12 point font (Garamond), making it very easy to read.

Titles and rubrics have been kept to an absolute minimum, leaving the page uncluttered, with the focus on the spoken words.

A generous margin and plenty of white space make the page inviting and easy to follow, even if it is a little unadventurous.

Care over the line breaks in the confession has ensured that the whole prayer fits on the page without losing the proper sense of the words.

WELCOME

Stand
HYMN

In the name of the Father, and of the Son,
and of the Holy Spirit. **Amen.**

The Lord be with you
and also with you.

COLLECT FOR PURITY *remain standing*

**Almighty God,
to whom all hearts are open,
all desires known,
and from whom no secrets are hidden:
cleanse the thoughts of our hearts
by the inspiration of your Holy Spirit,
that we may perfectly love you,
and worthily magnify your holy name;
through Christ our Lord. Amen.**

CONFESSION

God so loved the world that he gave his only Son Jesus Christ to save us from our sins, to be our advocate in heaven, and to bring us to eternal life. Let us confess our sins, in penitence and faith, firmly resolved to keep God's commandments and to live in love and peace with all.

Kneel **Almighty God, our heavenly Father,
we have sinned against you and against our neighbour,
in thought and word and deed,
through negligence, through weakness,
through our own deliberate fault.
We are truly sorry and repent of all our sins.
For the sake of your Son Jesus Christ, who died for us,
forgive us all that is past;
and grant that we may serve you in newness of life
to the glory of your name. Amen.**

Example 2 – How *not* to do it!

This example from an all-age service shows how *not* to do it. Can you spot the instances of bad practice? What would you do to improve it?

The text is a good size and there is plenty of white space on the page. Rubrics are in small italic and easily distinguishable from the text.

What is missing is a set of clear headings to help the congregation to see the shape and flow of the service.

Underlining has been used instead of proper titles. This results in an emphasis on the two songs, the reading and the 'Gifts'!

The following example shows the difference that some headings and one or two other changes can make …

We stand for the start of the service:

This is the day that the Lord has made.
Let us rejoice and be glad in it.

SONG 1

We kneel or sit to confess our sins together:

**Father,
we have sinned against heaven and against you.
We are not worthy to be called your children.
We turn to you again.
Have mercy on us,
bring us back to yourself,
as those who once were dead
but now have life through Christ our Lord.
Amen.**

God who is both power and love,
forgive you and free you from your sins,
heal and strengthen you by his Spirit,
and raise you to new life in Christ our Lord. **Amen.**

We stand to praise God:

O Lord, open our lips;
and our mouth shall proclaim your praise.

SONG 2 (Our GIFTS to God will be taken up as we sing.)

We thank you, Father, for all that we have,
for everything in heaven and on earth is yours.
All things come from you,
and of your own do we give you. Amen.

We sit for a READING which is followed by the response:

This is the word of the Lord.
Thanks be to God

Example 3 – Example 2 with a facelift

The spoken text has been moved right, giving a wider left margin. The page has retained its spacious feel, but the space has been better used, with the text more central.

Headings have been inserted (in a sans serif font – Gill Sans MT, bold) and the songs are indicated with a slightly smaller version of the same font.

Rubrics are in the same font, but in italic to distinguish what is said from everything else on the page. The use of headings has made it possible to simplify the rubrics.

In this case the new design has taken up slightly more space. If we needed to save that space we would have to look at the possibility of making some of the spaces between items smaller, or combining some of the lines of the prayers. Other options include omitting the text of the absolution, or making it much smaller.

Greeting

Stand This is the day that the Lord has made.
Let us rejoice and be glad in it.

Song

Confession

Kneel or sit

Father,
we have sinned against heaven and against you.
We are not worthy to be called your children.
We turn to you again.
Have mercy on us,
bring us back to yourself,
as those who once were dead
but now have life through Christ our Lord. Amen.

God who is both power and love,
forgive you and free you from your sins,
heal and strengthen you by his Spirit,
and raise you to new life in Christ our Lord. **Amen.**

Stand

Praise

O Lord, open our lips;
and our mouth shall proclaim your praise.

Song

During the song the offering will be taken.

We thank you, Father, for all that we have,
for everything in heaven and on earth is yours.
All things come from you,
and of your own do we give you. Amen.

Sit

Example 4

Here is a very different sort of approach, with an even more light and spacious feel, a large sans serif font for the spoken text, and 'friendly text' in boxes attached to the headings.

Text has been kept to a minimum. It could have been made even simpler by omitting 'Priest', 'All' and instructions. As it is, the page is so simple that they don't dominate or add to the clutter. Note that there is no need for colons after 'Priest' and 'All'.

Section numbers have been included, as has a page number.

Headings, rubrics and main text are all in Lucida Sans. The text in the boxes is Carolina.

1 The Greeting

We say, 'Hello'

Priest The Lord be with you.
All **And also with you.**

2 The Penitential Rite

We say, 'Sorry'

The Priest invites everyone to confess their sins.

All **Almighty God, our heavenly Father,**
we have sinned against you
and against our neighbour,
in thought and word and deed,
through negligence, through weakness,
through our own deliberate fault.
We are truly sorry and repent of all our sins.
For the sake of your Son Jesus Christ,
who died for us,
forgive us all that is past;
and grant that we may serve you
in newness of life
to the glory of your name. Amen.

Priest Almighty God,
who forgives all who truly repent:
have mercy upon you,
pardon and deliver you from all your sins,
confirm and strengthen you in all goodness,
and keep you in life eternal.
All **Amen.**

1

Example 5

In this example the font used throughout is Abadi. It gives a very clear distinction between ordinary text and bold text. Headings have been put in all capitals to distinguish them from the text for the congregation. An alternative would be to use a different font and lower case.

Section numbers have been used discreetly, in a smaller size and in the margin.

The simple icon of the book helps to show what is going to happen and signals visually that the most significant thing on this page is the reading of the Scriptures.

The header down the left-hand side is a little dominant, but acts as a constant reminder of which section of the service we are in.

Note that the silence after the first reading has been included as an element in its own right, not as a rubric.

Proclaiming the word of God

6 FIRST BIBLE READING

At the end of the reading this response is used:

This is the word of the Lord.
Thanks be to God.

SILENCE FOR REFLECTION

Stand

7 GOSPEL READING

The reader announces the reading and then uses this response:

Hear the gospel of our Lord Jesus Christ
according to *N.*
Glory to you, O Lord.

After the reading this response is used:

This is the gospel of the Lord.
Praise to you, O Christ.

8 THE SERMON

The sermon may be followed by a time of silence.

HYMN or SONG

Example 6

This example shows a simple two-column layout for a version of Night Prayer for St Gertrude's youth group.

To save space and to make a clearer distinction between the two, the text for the leader is one point smaller than that for the congregation.

There are no rubrics, as all instructions about posture, etc. are announced.

Section numbers have been included.

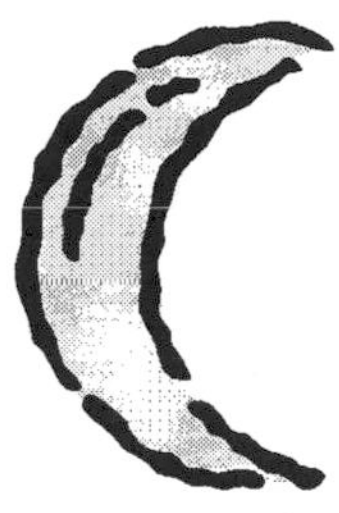

Night Prayer

- debriefing the day with God

St Gertrude's - 1 April 2000

1 Introduction: why are we here?

May the Lord almighty grant us a quiet night and a perfect end.
Amen.

Be swift, O God, to save us.
Come quickly, Lord, to help us.

May the angels of God guard us
through the night,
and quieten the powers
of darkness.

May the Spirit of God be our guide
to lead us to peace and to glory.

2 Confession: dishing the dirt on ourselves

Lord, we have wounded your love.
Merciful God, forgive us.

We stumble in the darkness.
Light of the world,
show us the way.

We forget that we are your temple.
Spirit of God, dwell in us.

Let's bring our darkness to God's light:
Most merciful God,
we confess to you
before the whole company
of heaven
that we have sinned
in thought, word and deed,
and in what we have failed to do.
Forgive us our sins,
heal us by your Spirit
and raise us to new life in Christ.
Amen.

If we confess our sins,
God is faithful and just,
and will forgive our sins,
and cleanse us from all unrighteousness.
Amen. Thanks be to God.

3 Jubilate (Psalm 100): praising God together

Cry out to the Lord, all the earth;
serve the Lord with gladness;
come into his presence
with songs of joy.

Be assured that the Lord is God;
he has made us for himself.
We are his own, his people,
the sheep who feed on
his pasture.

Example 7

This example shows one way of laying out options within the main text. The right hand margin is used for explanatory teaching comments and for instructions, leaving the main text of the service free of any rubrics.

Notice the use of a running header at the top of the page showing which section of the service we are in, and the footer at the bottom giving the title of the service and a page number.

Headings and explanatory notes are set in Gill Sans MT, the main text in Garamond.

Greeting

A Grace, mercy and peace
from God our Father and the Lord Jesus Christ
be with you
and also with you.

B Alleluia! Christ is risen.
He is risen indeed. Alleluia!

C The Lord be with you
and also with you.

Prayer of preparation

A Almighty God,
to whom all hearts are open,
all desires known,
and from whom no secrets are hidden:
cleanse the thoughts of our hearts
by the inspiration of your Holy Spirit,
that we may perfectly love you,
and worthily magnify your holy name;
through Christ our Lord. Amen.

B Lord, direct our thoughts,
teach us to pray,
lift up our hearts to worship you
in Spirit and in truth,
through Jesus Christ. Amen.

C Loving Lord,
fill us with your life-giving,
joy-giving, peace-giving presence,
that we may praise you now with our lips
and all the day long with our lives,
through Jesus Christ our Lord. Amen.

GATHERING

STAND

The president greets the people. The second greeting is always used in the 50 days between Easter and Pentecost.

The first of these is known as the ***Collect for Purity****. It was used in the Middle Ages as part of the clergy preparation before the service.*

The other two are newer and simpler prayers.

All three remind us that we need God's Spirit to pray and worship as God desires.

Example 8

In this example a very simple design has resulted in a very pleasing effect. There are lots of rubrics, but being in the same font as most of the rest of the page, they do not obtrude too much.

The secret is the use of fairly small text (Book Antiqua 10 point) and relatively large spaces between the blocks of text and rubric.

Though the small print size might cause problems for some, the result is a page with lots of white space on it.

There is plenty of room for a well-chosen piece of clip art to the right of the confession.

The absolution is split across two pages, but as this is a left-hand page the text continues at the top of the facing page and no page turn is required.

If this was a right-hand page it would probably be worth the attempt to fit it onto the page (or to omit the text and indicate it by rubric instead), though as it is not a congregational prayer it could be split if absolutely necessary.

THE GATHERING

STAND at the sound of the bell.

***A Hymn** is sung as the ministers enter and the altar is honoured with incense.*

The Greeting

All may make the sign of the cross, and the presiding priest greets the people.

Priest + In the name of the Father, and of the Son, and of the Holy Spirit.
All **Amen.**

Priest Grace, mercy and peace from God our Father
and the Lord Jesus Christ be with you.
All **and also with you.**

The priest adds words of welcome and introduction.

The Prayers of Penitence

The Deacon invites the people to recall and confess their sins. After a few moments of reflection, all say the prayer of confession.

All **Most merciful God,**
Father of our Lord Jesus Christ,
we confess that we have sinned
in thought, word and deed.
We have not loved you with our whole heart.
We have not loved our neighbours as ourselves.
In your mercy
forgive what we have been,
help us to amend what we are,
and direct what we shall be;
that we may do justly, love mercy,
and walk humbly with you, our God.
Amen.

President Almighty God,
who forgives all who truly repent,
have mercy upon you,

Index